# Social Research Perspectives

## Occasional Reports on Current Topics

10

# Your Time Will Come:
## The Law of Age Discrimination and Mandatory Retirement

by Lawrence M. Friedman

RUSSELL SAGE FOUNDATION   NEW YORK

# The Russell Sage Foundation

The Russell Sage Foundation, one of the oldest of America's general purpose foundations, was established in 1907 by Mrs. Margaret Olivia Sage for "the improvement of social and living conditions in the United States." The Foundation seeks to fulfill this mandate by fostering the development and dissemination of knowledge about the political, social, and economic problems of America. It conducts research in the social sciences and public policy, and publishes books and pamphlets that derive from this research.

The Board of Trustees is responsible for the oversight and general policies of the Foundation, while the immediate administrative direction of the program and staff is vested in the President, assisted by the officers and staff. The President bears final responsibility for the decision to publish a manuscript as a Russell Sage Foundation book. In reaching a judgment on the competence, accuracy, and objectivity of each study, the president is advised by the staff and a panel of special readers.

The conclusions and interpretations in Russell Sage Foundation publications are those of the authors and not of the Foundation, its Trustees, or its staff. Publication by the Foundation, therefore, does not imply endorsement of the contents of the study. It does signify that the manuscript has been reviewed by competent scholars in the field and that the Foundation finds it worthy of public consideration.

NOTICE of series title change: *Social Research Perspectives* is a new title for the *Social Science Frontiers* series (volumes 1–9 published 1969–1977). The numbering of *Perspectives* volumes is a continuation of the *Frontiers* numbering.

Library of Congress Catalog Number: 84-60650
Standard Book Number: 0-87154-295-1
10 9 8 7 6 5 4 3 2 1

# Social Research Perspectives

## Occasional Reports on Current Topics from the Russell Sage Foundation

The *Social Research Perspectives* series revives a special format used by the Russell Sage Foundation for nine volumes published from 1969 to 1977 under the series title, *Social Science Frontiers.* The *Frontiers* series established itself as a valuable source of information about significant developments in the social sciences.

With the re-named *Perspectives* series, we again provide a timely, flexible, and accessible outlet for the products of ongoing social research—from literature reviews to explorations of emerging issues and new methodologies; from summaries of current policy to agendas for future study and action.

The following *Frontiers* titles are still available:

5  *The Corporate Social Audit*, by Raymond A. Bauer and Dan H. Fenn, Jr. (1972)

7  *Social Forecasting Methodology: Suggestions for Research*, by Daniel P. Harrison (1976)

8  *The Vulnerable Age Phenomenon*, by Michael Inbar (1976)

9  *Work and Family in the United States: A Critical Review and Agenda for Research and Policy*, by Rosabeth Moss Kanter (1977)

# Contents

# Introduction

This is the account of a field of law which is mainly (though not entirely) about problems of old and middle-aged people. The "field" in question is age discrimination and its corollary, the law about mandatory retirement. More generally, it is about what happened in the law as this field emerged out of the primal void, so to speak. It is also about the process of making (and applying) rules.

Normally, new law begins with a distinctive social problem—air pollution, the crime wave—which exists either in the real world or in people's heads, or both. Age discrimination has a somewhat different character. It is fairly certain that there is a problem here, and in many ways it is a serious one. But no one is sure of its exact contours; and some have argued that the legal interventions here are related (or unrelated) in rather curious ways to the social background. In any event, a body of law did emerge, and crystallize into a "field," which, most emphatically, set certain forces in motion.

This is also a story about what we might call "legalization": a process in which "law" spreads its tentacles into problems,

1

situations, events, and areas of life where it had never penetrated before, or penetrated only in a most imperfect way. In recent years, there has been much discussion of this process. Something seems to be happening in society, and in the legal system, which is producing an outburst of law. The outburst takes many forms. Some people feel there is a "litigation explosion"—too many people suing each other. It is not at all clear whether the figures bear this out, in general; and it is not clear exactly what "litigation" means.[1] But *federal* cases do seem to be rising much faster than population.[2] Age discrimination cases are mostly federal; they are a small but growing part of the federal "explosion."

There is a lot of myth and humbug about the role of law and the amount of suing in society. Still, feelings about this subject are an important social fact. Many people feel we are suffering from too much law, or at least too much government. Article after article in the popular press complains about the overload— too much law, too many lawsuits, and lawyers; too many rules and regulations. Ronald Reagan's election in 1980 owed something to this feeling; and even liberals talk about cutting back the government. It is more than a matter of taxes. It is a belief that society is staggering under the sheer weight of rules.

Yet "legalization" has its good side as well. One aspect, after all, is the so-called "rights revolution" with its cousin the "due process" revolution. These terms refer, among other things, to advances toward equality and social justice. There have been rapid, amazing changes in practice and law over the last generation, increasing the rights of racial minorities—and of prisoners, school children, and mental patients, for that matter. Many of the changes have been, of course, quite controversial; some people grumble that we have gone too far or too fast; on the whole, nobody wants to go all the way back.

The "due process revolution" is a more complex and controversial form of legal change. Like "legalization" it is hard to describe and define precisely. It refers to a vast expansion of rights, especially procedural rights. The core idea is something along these lines: neither government nor any private power center should be able to take actions that affect a person's vital interests (the constitutional phrase is "life, liberty, or property") without "due process." This means (at least) telling that person about it in advance ("giving notice") and affording him a chance

2

to argue his side of the issue, together with a decent, genuine crack at fighting back.

Basically, this is a revolt against concentrated power—whether it is power in Washington or city hall; or the power of General Motors; or the power of a big hospital in Phoenix, Arizona. There is a general refusal to accept uncontrolled discretion. Lawsuits, statutes, and the general atmosphere of due process have worked together to transform the structure and life of institutions. In companies, schools, hospitals, prisons—in every organization, as well as in government itself—discretion has been limited, informal norms have stiffened into tough rules and regulations; offhand, informal processes have given way to procedures more or less like those in courts. Where there were no norms at all, or very informal ones, we now have rules of law.

There are dozens of examples of this process at work in modern life. For example, there was a time when a boss could hire and fire as he pleased, whom he pleased, when he pleased. Generally speaking, he could pay what he (or the market) decreed and run his business exactly as he liked. This is certainly no longer true—not for a company of any size. Today the boss is hemmed in by a massive network of rules. Government has forced these on him by and large—rules about overtime pay, about employee bathrooms and cafeterias, about the minimum wage, about "affirmative action." In many industries, union pressure led to major change in the structure of work relationships; but the unions of course have the force of law (and the National Labor Relations Board) behind them, at least since New Deal days. Labor relations, in short, have been thoroughly "legalized" over the years.

The workplace is not the only legalized domain. "Legalization" of schools is equally dramatic. Of course, public schools were always public, that is, always creatures of law. But the formal law paid only glancing attention to the day-by-day work of the schools. Today, rules about segregation, handicapped children, sex discrimination, bilingual education—the list could go on—have transformed the legal climate of at least the bigger school districts. Teachers, principals, school boards, have all suffered losses to their authority (in theory at least), partly under the pressure of litigation. The lost power has gone, to some degree, partly to students and others who were once without any say in the government of schools. Prisons and hospitals have traveled along a similar road. The judge who, in 1872, called prisoners "slaves of the state" would be amazed at "prisoners' rights" as they exist today.[3] It is important not to exaggerate this development (prisoners are still prisoners); but some reallocation of power has definitely taken place.

The focus in these pages is on two closely related subjects. Part I is about age discrimination; the legal status of mandatory retirement is the subject of Part II. Both of these topics are, of course, important in their own right, legally and socially; they are also prime examples of legalization. Forty years ago, there was virtually no such thing as the law of age discrimination. The very concept was almost unknown. If an employer wanted to get rid of everybody in his shop or factory over 50, or hire nobody over 40, as a matter of principle, only the market restrained him, if at all. This of course is no longer true. The legal status of forced retirement was also untouched by law until recent time. It was at most an issue for collective bargaining—and even there it is not very old.

I will begin with age discrimination. Age discrimination, as we have said, is legally the merest baby. Its origins do not go back very far—basically, one generation. It is, however, a lusty, healthy baby; it shows every sign of vigor and long life.[4] Yet, as shall be seen, it is a rather curious field of law. In part, it is about the elderly and their problems; but "age discrimination" as such does not refer to the elderly alone. On the contrary: "age discrimination," as a legal tool, is most useful for middle-aged people—those over 40 but under 70. Other aspects of the law of age discrimination apply to people of *any* age—20 or 30 or 80—odd as this may seem.

This essay begins with a brief description of the historical background of the law. The main focus is on *impact*. A "field" of law can be important for ideological or symbolic reasons; but surely its effect on the way people live, on the economy, and on social relationships is the heart of the matter. Alas, very little is known about impact, and there are few techniques for learning much. Speculation, of course, is always possible. The "field" of age discrimination also has an effect on the legal order itself. This, too, is important. Here impact can be traced more directly; conclusions about legal change, and their social implications, are here grounded more firmly in fact.

4

# Part I  Age Discrimination

## The Historical Background

In 1967, Congress passed the Age Discrimination in Employment Act (ADEA). In this law, the federal government created an important new legal mechanism. Later, in 1975, Congress passed another important law, the Age Discrimination Act (ADA).[5] Before these two laws, there were federal laws *about* the elderly, or which had an impact on them; but no law was concerned with "age discrimination" as such. There were, however, a number of state laws, some as old as the 1950s, or older, which made "age discrimination" illegal.[6] These laws, it is fair to say, did not make much of a splash at the time.

What lay behind ADEA, ADA, and the various state statutes? Here a few conceptual knots must be untied. There is, in the first place, the rather curious notion of "age" discrimination, meaning discrimination against *anybody* because of age, regardless of what that age might be—12, 40, 80, or 100. This notion crops up in ADA and in some state laws, but it is hard to find much of a history behind it. It is even harder to find a political movement or base. After all, everybody has *some* age.

A more important strand is the one which takes "age" to have a more specific meaning. Basically, "age" refers to the group called the elderly, or old people, or senior citizens. The elderly are just about the only *organized* group that has political significance and defines itself in terms of age. (Of course, there are other groups which are in effect age groups—veterans are an important example, historically. They tend to be from a single age cohort. But they do not *define* themselves exclusively in terms of age.) "Gray power" has a direct bearing on retirement law; but the relationship to discrimination laws is, frankly, obscure. ADEA does not apply to old people at all. As originally worded, nobody over 65 was covered.

There is, however, *some* relationship between the elderly and these laws; and the relationship is getting stronger. ADEA was amended in 1978 to include people over 65 but under 70. There is now a concerted effort to pop the cap off the bottle entirely and extend the act to everybody over 40, even 90-year-olds. These efforts might succeed nationally some day; they have already succeeded in a number of states. This would mean the end of mandatory retirement, which the "gray lobby" most definitely wants. A point or two about this interest group is therefore in order.

The first point is that the elderly have *become* an interest group only recently, in the twentieth century. Senior power reflects, first of all, certain massive social facts about the "graying of America." The demographics are, in general, well known. Modern sanitation and medicine allow people to live much longer than they did in earlier times. People over 60 are a significant group in America, in sheer numbers, and as a percentage of the population. By 1980, it is said, more than 35 million people in the country were 60 or older.[7] The percentage in this category has been rising faster than population in general. Meanwhile, the birthrate has gone down. The political and social power of younger people will decline in coming years, while the wants and needs of the elderly take on extra political urgency.

But of course sheer masses of people do not make law; neither do "problems" in the abstract. Pressure makes law. There has to be some sort of exertion, some sort of initiative. Laws are not immaculately conceived. Law-making bodies—including the courts—are reactive, not proactive. A legislature does not sit around thinking up statutes. Proposals come, in the main, from outside. They need an interest group to get them going.

6

An interest group is a collection of people who see themselves as having some problem or problems in common, and who are willing to take action to solve those problems. Mostly, the problems are economic or social: steelworkers and steel companies worry about imported steel; blacks worry about race discrimination. Mostly, too, the problem "belongs" to the people who push for a solution: auto workers or Chinese-Americans or farmers. Sometimes, the problem belongs to a wider public—to consumers, or even to the entire population. (At least, this is what consumer groups and environmentalists claim.) Still other interest groups focus on problems that "belong" to somebody else (battered children, for example, or people in prison).

For the sake of clarity, it might be good to draw a line between *reform* and *interest* groups. An interest group is concerned with its own problems, a reform group with somebody else's. There are, or certainly can be, important differences between the two types. Concretely, reformers might have ideas about what their clients want or need which are not at all the same as their clients' ideas. That is, prison reformers may fight for "reforms" that prisoners themselves do not particularly want, and vice versa. Many social movements are founded by reformers, then taken over by interest groups, or become a mixed bag. To a certain extent this has been true of the elderly. But whatever the background, the elderly are now an interest group in their own right and have been for some time past.[8]

An interest group begins, and keeps going, as was said, out of some sense of shared problems. Redheads are not an interest group. They have no common problems (or do not see any). Fat people are also not an interest group. (They may yet become one.) They recognize common problems, perhaps, but although they may diet together, they take no steps to organize for collective political action. An interest group does not need to include all or most of the people who share the problem. Most women are not active feminists. The few who are make up a powerful interest group.

During most of American history, the elderly as such were politically inert. No significant movements or political parties hinged their appeal on old people, middle-aged people, or *any* specific age group. Dramatic changes took place during the Great Depression of the 1930s—a period when many movements boiled up out of hunger and despair. One of these was the so-called

7

Townsend movement, founded by Dr. Francis E. Townsend; and its explicit focus was on older citizens.[9] Townsend's base was in California, that fertile source of delusion or innovation, depending on how one sees it. Townsend had a plan: pensions of $200 a month, starting at age 60, for everyone. The pensioners would retire on this money; and they had to spend every penny of it, every month. The plan was "always billed as an economic cure-all, rather than merely a program to provide handouts for aged Americans."[10] Ultimately, despite much noise, a national network of clubs, and some attempts at public office, the movement sputtered out.

The Townsend plan had a number of interesting features. We notice at once the Faustian bargain: money in exchange for jobs. The elderly would get out of the job market. Society would pay. In the depths of the depression, this did not look like a bad idea. There were no jobs anyway, and any plan that promised to spread the work was extremely appealing.

A similar bargain, of course, lies at the heart of one of the New Deal's most notable (and durable) achievements: the Social Security Act, or, more specifically, "social security," in the popular sense, that is, the old-age pensions which were part of the act. The law did not actually force anybody to retire; but old-age payments were restricted to people over 65 who had retired (or at any rate had no earned income).[11] Any pensioner who "received wages with respect to regular employment after . . . sixty-five" would forfeit some benefits: one month's benefit for every calendar month "in any part of which such regular employment occurred."[12] This provision had two effects—it gave magical significance to age 65 as the "transition point into old age"[13]; more significantly, it tended to force older workers off the job market.

There have been many changes in the act since 1935, but the core of it remains intact—including this aspect. In 1950, an amendment fixed the "exempt age" at 75. That is, a worker over 75 could work and not lose any benefits. (Those who went back to work after ten years in a rocking chair seemed to pose no threat to younger workers.) In 1954, the "exempt age" was reduced to 72.[14] In 1977, the "exempt age" was further lowered to 70; this change did not take effect until 1982.[15]

Behind these changes, of course, were years of argument and struggle. There has been pressure to lower the "exempt age," because the act is unfair (some say) to older people who want to work. There has been argument over whether we, as a society, want to encourage or discourage retirement. This argument has gotten more heated, in recent years, because of the financial crisis, the chance that the system will "go broke." But one point remains quite clear. Here, at the very center of the welfare state, is an example of what one *might* call age discrimination. The old-age pension is keyed to retirement. To get your money, you must leave the job.

Of course, this is "age discrimination" only in the sense that mandatory retirement is. (This issue is dealt with in Part II.) The retirement condition, under Social Security, has been (as one expert put it) "a continuing political irritant."[16] But it has its logic. Social Security is tied to wages, not to income in general. A man or woman of 65 can collect millions in rents or dividends and not lose a penny of the pension.[17] The elderly must clear out and make way for younger workers. By law, the payments were earned on condition. Jobs belonged, first and foremost, to the young.

Thus it is possible to label Social Security—unfairly, perhaps—as an instance of age discrimination. Not that people generally saw it that way—any more than women in 1900 looked on protective laws as "sex discrimination," though this they undoubtedly are from a modern standpoint.[18] The right to work your fingers to the bone when you are old and tired is like the right to be a woman coal miner. The right is real enough, and it is valuable; but one would hardly expect so subtle a consciousness in the middle of hard times. During the great depression, millions of people were struggling to survive, struggling to put bread on the table. The Social Security Act looked like a good deal, all things considered. Also, like certain other forms of "discrimination," it was in some ways meant as the opposite, that is, as benign: a package of benefits for a disadvantaged class. Each period looks at the world through a different lens.

Meanwhile, after World War II, Congress and the courts wrestled with civil rights, or, to put it more starkly, with the race question. Blacks made slow but steady progress in their struggle for legal and social equality. The Truman Administration issued an order finally desegregating the army. Black organizations kept up pressure in the courts for further progress; and the courts responded. In 1948, the Supreme Court struck down race-restrictive covenants (*Shelley* v. *Kraemer*)[19]; in 1954 *Brown* v. *Board of Education*[20] burst on the scene like a bombshell. Black voting power was growing in the North. In this period, too, some states passed "fair employment" laws.

Some of these, as mentioned earlier, went beyond race; they included religion, sex, and, occasionally, age. Age was added to the New York statute in 1958.[21] In 1959, the New York State Commission Against Discrimination reported that the law had had "salutary effects"; older workers enjoyed better job opportunities. Age discrimination accounted for 12.8 percent of the complaints filed that year with the commission (race accounted for 67.5 percent). The commission found "probable cause" in eighteen complaints. In one of them, for example, a county hospital refused to hire a cleaning woman who was 64; in another, a company told an engineering draftsman, who was 60, that "company policy" precluded hiring a man that old. Both these complainants got their jobs.[22]

By its own (perhaps biased) testimony, the commission was active, and doing good work, in the battle against age discrimination. The main event, quite properly, was race. And, of course, only a few states in the 1950s had fair employment laws to begin with (none of them in the South); only a minority of this minority covered age discrimination. As far as one can tell, age discrimination did not sit high on the agenda in any state commission. This was, as we said, only natural. The focus was on race.

Meanwhile, the gray lobby grew stronger. One concrete achievement was the Older Americans Act (OAA), passed by Congress in 1964.[23] This was a landmark: the first major federal law, since the Social Security Act, which prescribed a package of benefits for the elderly. OAA was part of the "Great Society" programs, Lyndon Johnson's cluster of domestic reforms. Like much of this program, it has persisted—amended many times and expanded greatly.

Even more important for the elderly were two health programs, Medicare and Medicaid. People were living longer, modern medicine was working miracles; but its "very successes in preventing and controlling diseases" bred problems. More and more people lived to 65 and thus became "susceptible to chronic and crippling conditions."[24] They—and the population as a whole—*believed* in medical miracles; they saw the market system as a barrier between them and their health. In the 1950s, there were loud demands for some way to help out with doctor and hospital bills. Medical costs were shooting up, along with medical opportunities. There was, to be sure, public assistance for the elderly poor; state and federal laws expanded these programs. But the strongest demand was for social insurance, to cover the middle class as well.

Medicare and Medicaid took the form of amendments to the Social Security Act, in 1965. Medicare was hospital insurance, administered through the Social Security system. It was linked to a voluntary, but subsidized, plan which let people buy insurance for doctor bills, too. Medicaid was for the poor: a program "to liberalize and extend the program of federal grants to states for the indigent and medically needy."[25]

Of course, the elderly desperately wanted these plans, especially Medicare. But the work of the gray lobby does not fully explain this success, after years of battle. Social arrangements were changing. Mom and Dad were living longer; they were not always welcome in their children's houses—if they had children—or if their children did not live far away. Middle-aged people, with old parents, faced a terrible dilemma: either to pay and pay, or neglect old Mother or Dad; or take them into their crowded house (and perhaps *still* pay and pay). Like Social Security, generally, Medicare lifted part of this burden from the backs of millions of people middle-aged and younger; it shifted the load to the government, and thus to taxpayers in general.

In general, one point emerges from the prehistory of age discrimination law. What the elderly wanted, as an interest group, was benefits. When these benefits benefited others, too, the elderly were successful. The historical record is bare of suggestions that the elderly as a group complained of "discrimination." The word "ageism" had not yet been coined in the 1930s or 1940s. Moreover, unlike Medicare, Social Security, and housing-for-the-elderly, which benefited the *children* of the elderly as well, "age discrimination" had a much more ambiguous status. In the job market, the age groups competed with each other; jobs for the elderly, except in a boom economy, meant jobs that might have gone to younger workers. Or at least younger

11

workers might look at it that way.[26] The history of retirement (see Part II) bears witness to this fact.

Nevertheless, by the 1950s, there were persistent complaints about job discrimination, complaints that people over 40 could not get jobs.[27] These complaints left their mark on Fair Employment Practices Commission (FEPC) laws in some states (for example, New York). Indeed, when the federal government entered the picture, it, too, restricted itself, at first, to *job* discrimination. And the state laws, like ADEA, had age ceilings. They were mainly in aid of the middle-aged; they excluded old people from the scope of their protection.

In other words, even after "age discrimination" entered the law, there were few complaints about general discrimination, and no general program. The matter began and ended with jobs (except for the benefit side). If we consider the history of black militance, which is centuries old, or the struggle for women's rights, which goes back to Seneca Falls (1848) and beyond—and if we consider what *kinds* of discrimination blacks and women have complained of, how pervasive they were or are, it is obvious that age discrimination is a social problem of a different order entirely.

Furthermore, the elderly continue to press for benefits, they continue (in other words) to argue against age neutrality. Billions and billions of dollars are paid out every year for old-age pensions, Medicare, housing for the elderly, services under OAA, to mention only the largest of the age-based programs.[28] According to one authority, there were forty-seven federal programs in 1977 that used age as a "major criterion for eligibility," one way or another.[29] The number of programs is growing all the time, along with other special benefits, large and small—including such local ones as lower bus fares for senior citizens. All of these convey a social message, which might be a wrong message, a stereotyped message, even a "discriminatory" message. (Compare the attitude staunch feminists take toward old-fashioned laws for "protecting" women.) How can one explain this rapid movement in opposite directions—*for* benefits, and yet *for* age neutrality? Are benefits some sort of reparation or payoff? If so, for what? What accounts for the way this field of law has developed?

We leap ahead to 1967, and the Age Discrimination in Employment Act.

The Age Discrimination in Employment Act was passed at the end of 1967.[30] It entered what was largely a statutory void, although there were prior executive orders (these did not apply to private businesses, unless they were working on government contracts).[31] Federally speaking, then, this was an important step in "legalization," in one primary sense of that term: legal norms were insinuated into an aspect of life that had been normless, or private, before. Of course other laws against discrimination had paved the way, conceptually speaking. Age discrimination was in part only an "add-on." This may explain why business took so little apparent interest. Nobody mounted a strong campaign against the law. By 1967, it was hard to be against "discrimination"; and earlier laws had already done most of the mischief, as far as red tape was concerned. Or so it seemed at the time.

ADEA, basically, created a new federal offense: age ⟶ discrimination. Under the law, it was illegal to refuse to hire a worker because of age, or fire a worker because of age. It was also wrong to discriminate, on the basis of age, in "terms, conditions, or privileges of employment" [sec. 4(a)(1)]. Parallel provisions applied to employment agencies and labor unions. Employers were covered if their industries "affected" commerce, and if they had twenty-five or more employees. The law was limited [sec. 12] to "individuals who are at least forty years of age but less than sixty-five." During debate, other bottom ages had been suggested. Some committee members were bothered by the way the airlines treated their stewardesses; these congressmen suggested ages as low as 32. Others suggested ages as high as 45; but age 40 won out.[32] For the upper limit, Congress chose 65, the "standard" age of retirement since the Social Security Act. Amendments in 1978 raised the upper age to 70.[33] The original text also contained some significant exceptions and a number of administrative provisions. Some of these will be discussed later on.

The political background of ADEA is surprisingly sparse. It was not the child of the lobby of old folks, although labor and the elderly did support it. But the law was not a law *for* the elderly as such. After all, nobody over 65 was covered at all. It was a law for the middle-aged; and while there are plenty of people in

13

this category, they hardly amount to an "interest group." They have no clubs or organizations; there are no lobbies for the middle-aged as such. (This does not mean, of course, that people over 40 are politically powerless, or that they do not exert pressure; they obviously do.)

On its face, ADEA is related to the civil rights laws of 1964. It borrows a good deal of their language. Most notably, it borrows the central concept: "discrimination." Whatever else was at issue, ADEA clearly bubbled up out of the general cauldron of civil rights, in some way or other. It looked like a natural step, in a period with civil rights on its mind. And there were, of course, precursors in the states.

The subject had indeed come up in 1964, during the debates over the Civil Rights Act. There were proposals to add age discrimination to the bill. Some congressmen and senators lamented the plight of the older worker, dumped on the trash heap, unable to find work. There is some reason to think that these were crocodile tears. The loudest backers of an age discrimination clause, somewhat suspiciously, were conservative Republicans and Southern Democrats. In the Senate, the proposal to add the word "age" lost 28 to 63; liberals voted no. It was the same in the House. Representative O'Hara (Illinois)—81 years old, and a liberal—was as opposed to age discrimination (he said) as anybody; but though the cause was good, "the timing is bad." Congress faced the job of getting rid of race discrimination; it was wrong to add "the ladies and the old people." If "you wrap them all in one package, three good causes will die on the vine."[34]

It is significant, however, that the basic complaint was about the job market. In fact, there was a good deal of discussion, before 1964, of the troubles of middle-aged and older workers in the job market. It was the subject of newspaper articles, letters to the editor, and some systematic studies and reports. One study, which covered 21,386 job openings listed with state employment offices in seven cities (1956), found that more than half of the jobs were closed to people over a certain age.[35] Nonetheless, the Civil Rights Act left age out. But Congress did not drop the matter entirely. The Secretary of Labor was ordered to "make a full and complete study of the factors which might tend to result in discrimination in employment because of age and of the consequences of such discrimination on the economy and individuals affected."

14

This was the first of several mandates to study and report—
on age discrimination, mandatory retirement, the impact of
age-sensitive laws, and so on. Reports are a good thing, one
supposes; but they sometimes suggest that nobody smells a crisis,
at least not an imminent one. (In a few rare cases—the Social
Security solvency question comes immediately to mind—the
crisis is so stark, the politics so risky, that *only* a nonpartisan
study may end up doing the trick.) Asking for reports also
suggests at times that nobody quite knows what to do. The report
device is also a common form of compromise. The law left "age"
out, but not because the liberals in Congress saw no point to a
law on the subject. In any event, Congress fixed a deadline: the
secretary was to publish his report no later than June 30, 1965.[36]

The report appeared as directed; and sure enough, it found a
problem. Society was full of age discrimination; something had to
be done.[37] The report perhaps acted as a catalyst. Bills on age
discrimination were introduced into both houses. On January 23,
1967, the President, Lyndon Johnson, endorsed ADEA, which
was pending in both houses. The law sailed smoothly through
Congress. The legislative history is exceedingly bland. ADEA
attracted little controversy. Debate was skimpy. Not a single
senator spoke against the bill, and only one congressman, who
perhaps thought the act did not go far enough. Representative
Eilberg mentioned the "social costs of age discrimination,"
which he said were "obvious." Apparently everybody agreed.
Representative Steiger bemoaned the fate of the elderly: "with
one hand," society does "everything possible to extend the life
span of man but with the other hand [it] throws him on the
industrial scrapheap . . . because of his chronological age."[38]
Nobody seemed to pay much attention to what was actually *in*
the law. Without much fanfare, the bill became law.

Little force, it seems, was *behind* ADEA; there was even less
huffing and puffing against it. If spokesmen of business saw the
law as a threat, they kept their mouths shut, relatively speaking.
Since the law in a sense came from nowhere, it is no surprise
that it came dressed in borrowed, analogical clothes. Its texture,
its form, its very language were derived from the laws on civil
rights. This is not the usual pattern for important legislation, but
it is hardly unique.

It is hard to explain ADEA, in general, in the way most major
laws *can* be explained: by pointing to the pull and haul of

15

well-defined, conventional interest groups. The legislative history does not show either a massive campaign *for* it; or a massive campaign *against* it (by business). Of course, the law did not slip into the world in the middle of the night, in secret. Obviously, there was enough social force behind it to get it enacted. It is a question of degree.[39]

To say that ADEA came out of nowhere, then, is of course not literally true. Yet the history of the law poses something of a paradox. ADEA produced a program now administered by a major federal agency. The agency handles thousands of complaints every year. There are hundreds of court cases on ADEA, and the numbers keep growing. Yet the law at least *seemed* to be some sort of virgin birth, or, perhaps more accurately, the unacknowledged child of mystery parents. This suggests some subtle social force at work, something other than loud braying in the lobby. I return to this point later on.

## The Federal Extension: ADA

In 1975, in a fit of absentmindedness (perhaps), Congress passed another law against age discrimination, which is called, appropriately enough, the Age Discrimination Act.[40] This was part of a package of amendments to the Older Americans Act, although ADA has little to do with older Americans. The amendments as a whole authorized about a billion and a half dollars, to be spent on various programs. ADA itself did not cost any money, and this may be why Congress paid so little attention. The amendments passed the House by a lopsided vote of 404 to 6, and in the Senate by 89 to nothing. Almost nobody criticized ADA, although Caspar Weinberger, Secretary of Health, Education and Welfare, complained in a letter that Congress had rushed ahead without resolving fundamental issues, that the statute set the country sailing on "wholly uncharted" seas, without any "specific legislative guidance." Many people think he had a point.

The arguments in Congress *for* ADA were hardly illuminating. They were mostly reruns of arguments for ADEA. One congressman talked about "staggering" unemployment "among older Americans" and the "fact" that "the older worker is too often the first to go and the last to be hired simply because of his age." (One would have thought ADEA took care of this problem.) Another congressman mentioned "evidence" that "the noninvolvement of the elderly in our society leads rapidly to their physical and mental deterioration."[41]

This evidence is real enough; but it is hard to connect it with ADA. The new law seemed to paint with a very broad brush. It applied to all federal programs and to programs and activities which received "federal financial assistance." No such program or activity could exclude anyone or discriminate against anyone "on the basis of age." The act also applied to "programs or activities receiving funds under the State and Local Fiscal Assistance Act of 1972."

One strange aspect of ADA was that it was not, in terms, confined to old or even middle-aged people. The key word was simply "age." The act applied, then, to young as well as to old, though the young played no part in the lobbying.[42] Obviously, it would be a disaster if Congress really meant what it said, if no program could "exclude" because of "age." Taken literally, this would mean that 5-year-olds might be eligible for Social Security, or that 80-year-olds could take advantage of funds available for dependent children or juvenile delinquents. No such things were of course intended.

What, then, *was* intended? The act originally spoke, in its statement of purpose, about "unreasonable" discrimination. The word "unreasonable" was dropped in 1978—after all, how can "discrimination" ever be "reasonable"?[43]—but the ghost of this thought still haunts the law. The act did not outlaw *all* age distinctions, but only some of them—the unreasonable ones. Indeed, the word "reasonable" remains part of the text. (Nobody, of course, talks about reasonable *race* discrimination, at least not now.)

There are age distinctions in every society; besides, such distinctions are deeply imbedded in American law. Hence it is no surprise that the drafters of ADA wrote certain "exceptions" into the law—exceptions so wide and vague that they almost swallow up the act. ADA exempts actions that "reasonably take into account age as a factor necessary to the normal operation . . . of the program or activity." Another exception allows "differentiation" if "based on reasonable factors other than age." A third exception [304(a)(5)(2)] states that the act does not apply to "any program or activity established under authority of any law" which provides "benefits or assistance" based on age or which uses age as a criterion. These phrases, obviously, exempt all (or almost all) public programs which draw an age line. The "benefits" exception, for example, clearly covers Social Security.

Beyond these exceptions, ADA says surprisingly little. As if aware of this fact, and the muddle it had made, Congress asked for yet another study, this time by the Commission on Civil Rights [sec. 307(a)]; it also asked the Secretary of Health, Education and Welfare to propose general regulations no later than one year after the commission's report or two and a half years after passage, whichever came first [sec. 304(a)(1)]. No doubt Congress hoped the regulations would give meaning to the act. The text most assuredly did not.

One might think that ADA was best left alone to simmer in its equivocal juices. But one short year later, Congress was at work again, passing a law which extended ADA (or perhaps not). This was an amendment to the State and Local Fiscal Assistance Act (SLFA), originally enacted in 1972. This act shovels out federal money to state and city governments and other local authorities. SLFA banned discrimination on the basis of race and so on; in 1976 Congress added "age" to the list. ADA prohibitions now also apply to any "program or activity of a State government or unit of local government" which receives funds under SLFA. To be sure, ADA had already covered "programs or activities receiving funds under the State and Local Fiscal Assistance Act." It is not clear whether the 1976 amendments added anything, or how the two acts are related, or whether they refer to each other out of politeness only. At any rate, there they are.

## And Still More Laws: ECOA and Others

By now, tacking the word "age" onto a list of forbidden factors had become almost a reflex action. In 1976, amendments to the Equal Credit Opportunity Act (ECOA) added still another important federal statute to the list. Under ECOA, a creditor must not discriminate in lending money "on the basis of race, color, religion, national origin, sex or marital status, or age (provided the applicant has the capacity to contract)."[44] The last proviso made clear, of course, that lenders do not have to deal with 15-year-olds, if they choose not to. (A minor is hard to

18

collect from, since he has no "capacity" to make contracts in the first place.)

Except for the "capacity" clause, ECOA (like ADA) simply uses the word "age," without saying *what* age it means. Thus this act, too, is not limited to the old. And it is no surprise to find sweeping exceptions in the text. One of these does concern the elderly: it is not discrimination to use an "empirically derived credit system which considers age," so long as this system is "statistically sound." However, the "age of an elderly applicant may not be assigned a negative factor or value" [15 U.S.C. 1691(b)]. (The regulations define as elderly anyone 62 or over.)

The act also excepts credit assistance programs "expressly authorized by law for an economically disadvantaged class of persons," or which are "administered by a nonprofit organization" [1691(c)]. Presumably, then, a program to extend credit to poor young mothers can turn down applications from old men, so long as the refusal is "pursuant" to the program.

As Howard Eglit has pointed out,[45] no federal law bans age discrimination in public accommodations (hotels, restaurants, and so on). Title II of the Civil Rights Act of 1964, which deals with the subject, does not list age among its forbidden discriminations. However, fourteen states (and the District of Columbia) do ban age discrimination in public accommodations. The Illinois law,[46] for example, covers people between 40 and 70. It applies to an enormous list of "places of public accommodation," including soda fountains, hat stores, shoe stores, public golf driving ranges, and ice cream parlors. One doubts that there has been a history of bigoted hat stores, whose owners chased out customers over 40. The Illinois act also applies to "funeral hearses, crematories, cemeteries"; these, alas, are all too hospitable to the elderly.

Almost certainly these laws are afterthoughts (as regards age); almost certainly they do not arise out of an acute sense of social injustice, or even any particular incidents—no screaming headlines about ageist hat shops. They do reflect a feeling that age is a bad criterion in many social situations. The laws keep coming, and some of them are quite significant. An amendment in 1974 extended ADEA to include federal and state employees —a large and important group of people.[47] (In 1983, the Supreme Court, by a razor-thin margin, held this amendment constitutional, as it applied to employees of states.[48]) The original act covered employers with twenty-five workers or more; the

1974 amendment dropped this to twenty. Even more significant was the ADEA amendment of 1978, which raised the age limit from 65 to 70. This not only added more customers, it also affected every retirement plan which fixed 65 as its basic age. Debates on this bill were, as one might expect by now, quite sparse; and they dealt mostly with the retirement issue.[49] The subject gets fuller treatment in Part II.

This then is the general state of the law. It is illegal to "discriminate" against workers between 40 and 70. It is illegal to "discriminate" in federal programs, and in federally supported programs, with regard to any age. The two basic laws have broad exceptions (ADA's are *very* broad). State law by now often tracks the federal laws. There are state and federal bureaucracies, charged with enforcing laws against age discrimination; there is also the live, active path of private lawsuits, at least under ADEA and some state laws.[50]

Administratively, and in most other regards, ADEA is far more important than ADA. There is no separate agency responsible for enforcing ADA.[51] The Department of Labor was originally responsible for ADEA. Under Carter's Reorganization Plan No. 1 of 1978, ADEA was transferred from Labor to the Equal Economic Opportunity Commission (EEOC).[52] ADEA had not made much of a splash at Labor. In the early 1970s, it commanded less than 5 percent of the staff and expenditures of the Wage and Hour Division.[53] In EEOC, ADEA cut a better figure. Eleanor Holmes Norton, who headed the agency, promised to give age discrimination the same billing as race and sex—"the exact equal in importance."[54] (This was probably a harmless exaggeration.) The Carter Administration, of course, went out of business, and the Reagan Administration is assumed to be less zealous. Whether this is so or not is unclear. The latest EEOC report—for fiscal 1982—is dry and matter-of-fact. But the volume of complaints is high. Total activity, administrative and judicial, has been rising all along; and the end is not in sight.

Americans see nothing odd about mixing public and private enforcement; they expect the right to bring their own lawsuits, even if public agencies turn down their cases. Not that a person with a grievance can go charging into court. Action under ADEA involves several procedural wrinkles. In general, a person who feels aggrieved has to meet two requirements before suing in federal court. At least sixty days before filing suit, he or she must bring a complaint of discrimination before EEOC. He or she must also begin state proceedings—at least if the state has its own law against age discrimination and can grant some sort of relief. (Such states are called "deferral" states.[55]) These requirements give EEOC a chance to work out a settlement, using conciliation, and to screen out complaints that could be resolved by state agencies.[56]

The law permits but does not favor lawsuits, either public or private. Under section 7b of ADEA, the government is ordered not to rush into court. Rather, it should try to eliminate "discriminatory practice" through "voluntary compliance," using "informal methods of conciliation, conference, and persuasion." Paradoxically, this section has been one of the major issues in litigation. A few courts have insisted that "conciliation, conference, and persuasion" are "jurisdictional prerequisites to filing suit."[57] Others disagree, or at least hold that conciliation is not "jurisdictional"; if the government has not tried hard enough to conciliate, the case can be stayed (not dropped) until the defect is corrected.[58] But *how* hard does the government have to try, before it goes to court? How much "informal" effort will do? And what does the effort consist of? These are difficult questions, and the case-law, though it struggles hard to come up with "guidelines" and "tests," does not really answer the question.[59]

The relationship between conciliation and enforcement also raises something of an issue. Criminal statutes do not usually allow conciliation. A first-time violator is (in theory) just as guilty as a repeater and is liable to be punished. A company that violates ADEA, however, gets one free bite of the apple. A knowing violator can take a chance on getting away with this "crime"; the worst it faces is "conciliation," coughing up back pay and promising to sin no more. Only stubborn companies face lawsuits, tough injunctions, and the like.

This is theory. In practice, conciliation and other informal methods are common everywhere, including criminal law, even when official law does not recognize them. Despite the emphasis on conciliation, severe sanctions—back pay amounting to millions in a few cases—*have* been imposed on some violators. A division of Standard Oil agreed to pay $2 million to various employees. The Department of Labor went to some lengths to publicize this case to put the fear of God into other employers.[60]

EEOC, like other agencies, prefers to settle and arrange. It goes to law only as a last resort and for strategic reasons. And, in theory, most problems can be handled in advance by telling the customers exactly what they are supposed to do. This is the function of the text of the law itself, and of the regulations which put flesh on its bones. The agency tries to sniff out problems before they arise, and presolve them through rules. (Other regulations get written as concrete questions arise). The process of writing "regs" is thus an important aspect of legalization.

ADEA's "regs," so far, are not particularly rich. Some phrases in the law almost cry out for expansion or explanation. For example, under the act, an employer cannot force workers out before they reach 70; there is an exception for those between 65 and 70, who, for two years at least, had been "employed in a bona fide executive or a high policymaking position" and were entitled to a pension of $27,000 or more. What is a "bona fide executive" and what does "high policymaking" consist of? The regulations quote (rather timidly) from the Conference Report. At least we learn, among other things, that "the chief economist or the chief research scientist of a corporation" is a "high policymaker"; and that "executive" does not mean "middle management," for example, "the head of a . . . warehouse or retail store" in a chain of stores (29 C.F.R. 1625.12).

Few regulations have given rise to litigation. This does not mean, of course, that they have no impact on the way agencies handle their problems and on the advice lawyers give to their clients. In any event, regulations go only so far. They can be challenged; and they do not cover all situations. The meaning of a new law is, in the largest sense, unpredictable. ADEA created a new concept. What impact the law would have was unknown. Unless a law is inert (a "dead letter"), courts, civil servants—and users generally—refine and define its meaning, test its edges, map out areas of conflict or consensus. Some of this defining may happen through litigation. Cases, after all, do not come out of the blue. Real people, who feel real grievances, bring them up. At some point, these people have consulted lawyers, who help them "transform" their grievances into claims.[61] Realistically, then, the public and its lawyers help define the meaning of law.

The number of complaints under ADEA, and its state equivalents, is constantly growing. It is part of the process of judicialization, and it is connected to what seems to be a growing American claims consciousness. The Department of Labor received about 1,000 complaints in 1969; in 1976 it received over 5,000. EEOC (the successor agency) received about 11,000 complaints in fiscal 1982.[62] State activity, too, moves steadily up. The number of lawsuits is also growing—suits brought by agencies and suits brought by private plaintiffs. The number of *reported* cases has increased dramatically since 1967. There is no doubt the word is getting around, at least among enough potential litigants to make a dent. A black woman over 40, fired from a job, has three possible grounds for complaint. A white male over 40 has one; he seems more likely to use it than he did before.

Cases and complaints are, in a sense, rare exceptions. Thousands of people over 40 apply for jobs every day; in thousands of cases, the employer hires a younger person instead. Every day, thousands over 40 get passed over or lose their jobs. Still, if even the tiniest fraction of these people complain, and a fraction of this fraction pushes its way into court, the result looks like a minor "explosion."

ADEA came to life, perhaps, in a somewhat casual way, but it has turned out to be an important shift in law. It gave power and privilege to middle-aged workers; it helped "legalize" age as a category.

Age was never, of course, legally irrelevant. Rights to vote, marry, or get elected to Congress all depend on age. Age makes people eligible (or ineligible) for many programs, such as Social Security. These bits and pieces never coalesced into any *general* principle. But after ADEA, and ADA, there seemed to be a rule, in effect, which made distinctions based on age suspicious if not downright illegal, at least in some aspects of life.

Did ADEA and ADA affect the job market? Did they change public attitudes toward age? Did they alter legal process? There are no clear answers to these questions. Enforcement agencies write annual reports; these tend to be self-serving. Reported cases, regulations, and other public sources are more or less biased. They are skewed toward behavior that evokes these legal responses. But a law and its surrounding behavior may make the biggest impact where it shows least, that is, in people's minds.

Causality, too, is a difficult puzzle, in trying to trace the impact of law. What was the effect of *Brown* v. *Board of Education* on race relations, for example? Surely it had *some* effect; but what made *Brown* possible in the first place were changes in race relations taking place in society, so that (from a certain standpoint) *Brown* itself and certainly what followed were as much effects as causes. One can even ask whether "cause" means anything in contexts like these.

A new law is, at best, only a blueprint. In a given legal culture it creates a structure or a plan for a structure. It also moves into a living, ongoing legal tradition. People in society react to or treat a new "law" in patterned ways. They have reacted before and will react again. Laws create opportunities, evoke expectations, touch off behaviors among professionals and laymen; these are always bounded and grounded by the social context.

There are "dead letter" laws that produce no impact, but most laws make some behavioral mark, inside or outside the legal system. Judges and administrators do something with the blueprints. So do members of the public, although this is often harder to see or to get at. Litigation is one sign of public impact. It is internal to the legal system, but it is also an indicator of external reaction. To be sure, litigation data must be used with caution. Cases deal with extremes, or they may be the tip of an iceberg. Of course, the bottom of an iceberg may be much like the top, only more so.

I will begin the discussion with an example of how *doctrine* fared under ADEA. The topic is the so-called BFOQ exception. This has evoked a small but interesting group of cases, which test the policy of the act. BFOQ leads us into a discussion of litigation brought by private citizens, one of the most obvious signs of ADEA's impact; then some treatment of the underlying social meaning of this litigation.

## BFOQ: An Essay on Doctrine

ADEA granted a general right to be free of discrimination in the job market (at least for those over 40 and under the ceiling age). The rights were not absolute. One exception, rather dimly drafted, concerned retirement plans. This is discussed in Part II. Another was the BFOQ exception. An employer can take age into account if age is a "bona fide occupational qualification," reasonably necessary to the "normal operation of a particular business."[63]

The language was not original. It was lifted from Title VII of the Civil Rights Act. In Title VII, BFOQ is a permissible defense against charges of sex discrimination or discrimination on the basis of religion and national origin.[64] (No BFOQ defense is allowed for race.) BFOQ has been a big issue in sex discrimination cases; it was in a sense an issue in the *Murgia* case (on early retirement of policemen), one of the Supreme Court's rare encounters with age discrimination.[65]

The underlying idea is simple enough. Men and women have different bodies; so do young and old. (What the BFOQ exception means in regard to religion or national origin is a different matter.) Since the differences are real, employers ought to be able to draw *some* line for *some* occupations. Where should the line be drawn? The answer is: where physical differences have a "bona fide" relationship to what the job demands.

Bodies, however, are only the starting point; body differences of sex and age lead to cultural differences, role differences, differences in the way people identify themselves, how they think of themselves and of others. These cultural differences between men and women, young and old, are also facts. We can make a lot, or a little, of these, as we wish. In short, BFOQ might be a big or a little exception; it might expand or contract; and the socio-legal effect of ADEA would expand or contract along with it.

In fact, agencies and courts have shrunk BFOQ to the merest remnant. Cultural differences are completely taboo. It is no defense, in a civil rights case, to refer to women's historic role in society or to traditional patterns of behavior. This means that BFOQ is a rare, difficult defense in sex discrimination cases. In age cases, too, the shrinking has gone quite far. One might argue, of course, that BFOQ should mean nothing at all in age cases. How can age ever be an "occupational qualification"? Suppose a job takes muscles and stamina. A company refuses to hire workers over 60. Almost everybody over 60 *might* find the job too hard. But age is not the BFOQ; strength is. Strength correlates highly with age—but not perfectly, just as it correlates (somewhat) with sex.[66] A rare man (or woman) of 63 might do the job—and why not let him? Why have a blanket rule? The very point of the act is to ban such blanket rules.

The sex discrimination cases came first, are better known, and set the tone. In general, an employer cannot use BFOQ as an excuse to lock men and women into traditional sex roles. Popular ideas about women's place in the work force will not be allowed to prevail. Nursing is not "women's" work, in such a way as to exclude male nurses. Coal mining, similarly, is not restricted to men. Nor do courts accept arguments that women are too weak, too slow, or too short for "men's" jobs. A company cannot keep women out merely because a job is "arduous." Women are not "physically unsuited" even for heavy work, which was always done by men. The Supreme Court upheld an Alabama prison regulation that excluded women from "contact positions" in men's prisons; but on the whole employers have lost most cases of BFOQ.[67]

Courts pay even less attention (as they should) to vague arguments about women's "nature" and psychology, which are supposed to make some jobs "unsuitable." In a New York case, one Bernice Gara wanted to become a baseball umpire. Umpires were supposed to be 5' 10" and to weigh 170 pounds. According to spokesmen for the baseball industry, these were not arbitrary standards, but "the judgment of men with long experience." The "size of professional baseball catchers," the "possibility of confrontation with big athletes," the physical strain of the game —these meant that umpires must be big and burly themselves: "a person who commands respect of big fellows, big men." The New York court turned down this stew of excuses.[68]

*Diaz* v. *Pan American Airways*[69] was an important federal case. *Diaz* broke the sex line for cabin attendants on airplanes. The airlines made a rather obnoxious argument: women, they said, were better than men at comforting passengers. (One psychiatrist explained that an airplane was an enclosed space; it perhaps reminded travelers of life in mother's womb.) Possibly on the grounds that one piece of nonsense deserves another, the court held that the argument about passenger comfort was beside the point, since, whatever it is that stewardesses (or stewards) did, it was not the "essence" of Pan American's business. The airline lost the case; and this ended the era of one-sex attendants.

BFOQ has been given a narrow meaning in age cases, too. This is foreshadowed in the regulations, which scrape up very few examples of legitimate use of BFOQ: "actors required for

28

youthful or elderly characterizations or products designed for, and directed to appeal exclusively to, either youthful or elderly customers." Even these categories were supposed to be "narrowly" construed; the employer must bear a heavy burden of proof [sec. 860.102b.d.e]. Aside from these rather trivial examples, the regulations mention only one significant instance: airline pilots. Here the issue is public safety, the only factor (so far) that has impressed the agencies and courts. Only here have courts given scope to BFOQ—indeed, perhaps too much.

Concern over public safety is only natural when the issue is airline pilots. Nobody wants pilots who have heart attacks high above mother earth. The risk is clearly greater for older pilots. Yet even here the argument almost proves too much. It would justify *any* line, past the most callow youth. Why not simply give stringent physical exams to airline pilots? (I leave to one side the technical argument that it might violate the law if pilots over 40 had to take tighter exams than younger pilots.) The answer is plain: physicals are not magic. Everybody has his own story of someone who dropped dead after passing a physical "with flying colors." At any rate, airline pilots are the most clear-cut case of BFOQ. The Federal Aviation Administration (FAA) has a limit of 60 for these pilots,[70] and courts have consistently upheld the limits,[71] despite opposition from the pilots themselves.[72]

The most important *cases* on BFOQ and age are not about pilots; they are about bus drivers. These cases did not concern retirement age, however; they focused on company rules against *hiring* people over a certain age. This was, of course, the social problem ADEA originally aimed at. In *Hodgson* v. *Greyhound Lines, Inc.* (1974),[73] the bus company refused to hire intercity drivers who were over 35. The defense, of course, was BFOQ, justified on grounds of safety. The court talked tough: defendant had to show that its restriction was "necessary," not just convenient or useful. But Greyhound was "entrusted with the lives and well being of passengers," hence safety was a "paramount goal." Greyhound did not have to show that "all or substantially all bus driver applicants" over 40 (the ADEA threshold age) could not perform safely; all it had to show was a "rational basis in fact to believe that elimination of its maximum hiring age will increase the likelihood of risk of harm to its passengers." Even "a minimal increase in risk of harm" was enough—if hiring older drivers meant danger to the life of a single extra person, compared with "the present hiring practice," then the cutoff age was fully justified.

Whether Greyhound had proved this danger was another question. The company dredged up material about the ravages of age, its "degenerative physical and sensory changes." But curiously enough, it was Greyhound, not the government, which trumpeted the fact that men in their 50s, men with sixteen to twenty years of experience, were the safest bus drivers. The argument was that drivers could not reach this "optimum blend of age and experience" unless they started young. (This assumes, of course, that it was experience that made veteran drivers so good, not the patterns of behavior characteristic of older people in our society.)

The government was willing to admit that the human body suffers, alas, "degenerative change" as the years roll on. But drivers over 40 could compensate through "increased maturity and driving experience." "Functional" age, not chronological age, was the proper test. There was also a mass of evidence about the work style of Greyhound bus drivers and about the "emotional stress" of driving. Interstate routes, it seems, were no picnic; they disrupted a driver's routine and complicated his home life. Under the seniority system, older drivers chose the best work deals for themselves; new drivers had to "accept whatever work is not performed by the regular drivers." This meant more difficult, stressful work—hence less safe. This, too, was an argument against hiring older drivers.

In the end, Greyhound won. The government (so the court felt) demanded too much "certainty"; its line of argument would require Greyhound to "experiment with the lives of passengers." (There was no other way to gather statistics on the safety record of drivers hired over 40, after all, than to put them on the job and let them roll.) The court decided not to disturb Greyhound's policies. The company had made a "good faith judgment" about passenger safety. The policies were not "arbitrary" or "lacking in objective reason or rationale."

*Usery* v. *Tamiami Trail Tours, Inc.*[74] was another bus case, decided two years later. The facts were quite similar. The company refused to hire drivers over 40. The court in *Tamiami* talked a different test, but reached the same general conclusions. Safety, said the court, was of the "essence" in the interstate bus business. This allowed the court to align itself with the *Diaz* case (on stewardesses). How one tells an essence from a nonessence was never explained.

The court did not stop there, however. The company had to do more than show that safety was an essence. It also had to show that everybody (or almost everybody) within the protected class (older workers) would be unable to do the job safely. This would never be easy, but the company could try to show, instead, that there was no practical way to test workers one by one, or deal individually with people over the age limit. This last point was a valuable escape valve; the company won its case.

This way of expressing the "test" of BFOQ has been more popular than the "test" in the *Greyhound* case. In *Arritt* v. *Grissell*,[75] for example, the court bought the *Tamiami* test, almost word for word. But this verbal formula does not mean the employer always wins. In *Arritt*, plaintiff wanted a job on the police force of Moundsville, West Virginia. He was 40 years old. Under West Virginia law, this made him too old to apply. The district court threw out his case. The Court of Appeals was more sympathetic. The burden was on the employer to show, first, that the age rule was connected to the "essence" of its business. He also had to show "reasonable cause . . . for believing that all or substantially all persons within the class" could not do the job; or (the escape valve) "that it is impossible or impractical to deal with persons over the age limit on an individualized basis." On these (rather cloudy) issues of fact, the case was sent back for trial.

*Arritt* v. *Grissell* was followed by a case about that sacred cow, the airline pilot. Gerald Smallwood, a pilot from Fairfax, Virginia, applied (at 48) for a job with United Airlines. He had flown jets for ten years with Overseas National Airways, which went out of business. United took applications from pilots between 21 and 35; 48 was much too old. The defense, of course, was BFOQ; but United lost.[76] *Arritt* v. *Grissell* was extensively quoted. United (the court felt) had not met its burden of proof. Yet the issue was basically this: when is safety an excuse for a cutoff age in hiring? United ran "extensive" tests on pilots—"blood screening, electrocardiograms, urinalysis, chest x-rays . . . diabetes screening." These tests would be just as "effective" on a "newly-hired 48-year-old pilot from another airline" as it would be for "career United pilots." Hence United had not shown a real connection between "a maximum age-at-hire limitation and airline safety." Obviously, Smallwood's experience with another airline distinguished the case from *Greyhound* or *Tamiami*; but the case did take a skeptical approach to safety rules.

Few jobs, of course, are like an airline pilot's, or a bus driver's, where, arguably, a sudden heart attack or slow reflexes puts passengers at risk. BFOQ in the case-law has affected only a tiny group of workers: pilots (air, bus, or river[77]), police, and firemen—that is just about all. In most other jobs, the worker himself is the only victim, if he collapses on the job. Hence, BFOQ is not a good argument, even when the job itself is quite dangerous. In *Houghton* v. *McDonnell Douglas Corp.*,[78] plaintiff was a test pilot, 52 years old. The company, squeezed financially, had to let some pilots go; it "decided to do so by age." Phillip Houghton was the oldest of the lot. The appeal court refused to accept BFOQ as a defense.

BFOQ, in other words, has shrunk considerably. Safety is the only important argument that seems to work; even here, the trends are mixed; there are signs of both vitality and constriction.[79] The general results make sense, legally and socially. They are in line with the logic of discrimination cases. Society and employers are entitled to demand strong fire fighters, laborers who wield a good shovel, typists who type fast and accurately. But since age does not disqualify *everybody*, the BFOQ excuse applies only when the possible effect on public safety, or some other public right, seems especially clear.

In a few states, people above a certain age who want to get or renew a driver's license face special requirements.[80] Apparently, this is legally acceptable. (There is at least a technical argument that these tests are unfair—"discriminatory"—under some state statutes.) The requirements seem better, or at least more just, than a flat, cruel rule chasing everybody off the road at 70, or even at 80. Some older people, even some who pass the tests, will have heart attacks; a few innocent bystanders (or drivers or passengers) will get hurt. Some old people may have accidents which younger people, with more nimble reflexes, could have avoided. But how many? The elderly may even be, on the whole, less accident-prone than the young; few old folks play chicken or drive drunk.

The same reasoning should apply to jobs. A fireman must be able to fight fires. An 80-year-old with arthritis and bad eyesight has no right to the job. But should the principle be any different for a 26-year-old fireman, who may be sick, flabby, dissolute, or disabled? Age, after all, does not disqualify in itself; it is only a surrogate or an indicator. Yet this is precisely the nub of the argument. Is it acceptable to use age in this way? Sex and race are forbidden. An age rule is cheap and easy to run; it is also unfair.

Businesses accept social stereotypes; they can hire and fire more efficiently (they feel) if they use a flat rule. The act, as interpreted, breaks through this pattern; it gives to older workers a new entitlement, the right to compete on the job market, free from "discrimination," whether or not the process saves or loses money for society. This is generally the case with "rights"— efficiency is not the be-all and the end-all. "Freedom of speech," for example, means (among other things) that religious quacks can pester and pursue millions of people in airports. "Due process" means tying the hands of police, or managers, or judges, at least to some degree.

In BFOQ cases, "discrimination" (in sex and age litigation) means behavior that conforms to older social stereotypes. The law is an attempt to smash these patterns. By doing so, the law acts as a lever, a focus, in an important social process. Of course, "the law" did not invent the attack on sex roles or age roles. It reflects changes going on in society and the struggle for further change. These changes are mirrored in the lawsuits people bring, which the next section of this essay discusses.

One key aspect of the law of age discrimination is the rapid growth of litigation. The law requires conciliation; but if conciliation fails, the agency can take an employer to court. Even more interesting is the growing volume of private litigation, cases in which plaintiff sues as an individual (or group), without agency help.

Most reported cases—there are hundreds of them—turn on points of procedure. This is not surprising. Reported cases are, in the main, appellate cases. Many of them involve points of administrative law. Actual facts are not good grounds for appeal, either from a lower court or from an administrative agency. This relegates the parties to arguments about whether one side or another took the right steps at the right time, under the law. In any event, the line between procedure and substance is not always clear, especially if "procedure" is defined to include questions of evidence and proof. A radical change in the working law can come about disguised as a shift in the burden of proof.

Proof problems are central to antidiscrimination law. Each type of case (race, sex, age) has its own wrinkle, of course, but there are common issues. The core concept ("discrimination") is the same. Basically this is a concept of intent, a concept of motive. It thus refers essentially to thoughts in somebody's mind, and it fits such "minds" as the University of Alabama or General Motors rather poorly. Evidence of "discrimination" tends to be circumstantial (and getting more so, as we shall see). Problems of proof, procedure, and fact-finding are at the heart of litigation practice.

To prove discrimination is more than a problem in technique. The trouble lies deeper, in the concept itself and in the mismatch between the shape of legal doctrine and the facts of social life. To explain this point, a bit of history is helpful. *Brown* v. *Board of Education* (1954) is a convenient starting point.[81] *Brown*, of course, was about segregated schools: separate systems for black and white children. Southern law, and the law of some border states, *required* separate schools. The Supreme Court, in its earlier incarnations, had upheld this segregated system.[82]

The *Brown* case itself did not waste many words on proof or intent. After all, segregated schools were not something the stork brought in; all over the South there were specific, definite, deliberate statutes demanding segregation; there was no question what they meant.[83] The first cases after *Brown* were also easy, at least in this sense. They dealt with segregation in public parks, swimming pools, and so on. Here, too, real, conscious, positive law kept the races apart.[84]

As the civil rights issue moved north, it faced more complicated issues. One began to hear about "de facto" segregation and more subtle forms of discrimination. Intent became, for the first time, a serious problem. It was by now obvious, South and North, that the Supreme Court (and the country) would never go back to Jim Crow. Even the diehards could see that. The civil rights laws of 1964 hammered the point home. Discrimination would have to go underground. The overt would give way to the covert. Any business that had documents, memos, rules, or even conversations that sounded "discriminatory" would be doomed to lose civil rights cases. Official policy in companies and agencies would have to change; and it did. In fewer and fewer instances would plaintiffs find a "smoking gun."

In the history of civil rights law, *Griggs* v. *Duke Power Co.* (1971) has been a pivotal case.[85] *Griggs* concerned the scope of the civil rights laws of 1964. The laws (said the Court) did not reach only "overt discrimination"; they also affected practices "fair in form, but discriminatory in operation." This launched what is called the "disparate impact" doctrine.

The core idea is this: plaintiff, in a discrimination case, can make a good first showing by bringing in evidence that defendant—a company, let us say—adopted a rule, or took some action, which hit blacks (for example) harder than whites. To show "disparate impact" does not mean that plaintiff automatically wins. But now the ball is in the company's court. It must explain its move, give a good reason for the rule or practice. Only in this way might it rebut the presumption that what it intended all along was the actual impact of its actions: to harm or exclude black workers.

*Griggs* itself was a case in point. Duke Power Company had a long history of race discrimination. Blacks were restricted to menial jobs. This practice of course became illegal. Suddenly, the company adopted new rules about job qualifications. Nobody could become a coal handler without a high school diploma. *Current* coal handlers (all white) were exempt from this requirement. The new rule cut off most blacks in the community, but very few whites. The company also suddenly saw a need for testing. The blacks at Duke Power, who all worked in the "labor" department, at low-paying jobs, were not allowed to transfer to better jobs unless they passed the Wonderlic Personnel Test, supposed to measure general intelligence, and the Bennett Mechanical Comprehension Test. Whites usually did well on these tests; local blacks tended to have less education, and usually failed.

The requirements, in other words, had "disparate impact"; they did more damage to black job-seekers than to whites. Once plaintiff proved this, the court challenged the company to show some reason, other than prejudice, to explain why the new rules were adopted. How come the new-born passion for tests? Were the tests "related to job performance"? The "touchstone" had to be "business necessity." If the company could not meet the burden, if it could not show that the tests measured something *directly* related to work, then the tests were illegal.

Disparate impact started out, then, in the *Griggs* case. It was perfectly justified there—anybody above the age of 5, reading the facts of the case, could smell blatant, obvious prejudice. The company was twisting and turning every which way to keep the good jobs for the whites. Tests appeared only after civil rights laws went into effect. Duke could hardly argue that those tests were a "business necessity"; they had never used them before.

"Disparate impact" is now recognized doctrine. How far it goes, where the boundaries are, what it means in detail—these are highly controverted questions. The doctrine has never been ruthlessly applied. Carried to its logical extreme, it would wreak havoc in the job market; for many jobs, a company's only safe course would be some sort of quota system. There is, it must be repeated, a crucial escape hatch. The company can show that a rule or test is "job-related"; this tosses the ball back to plaintiff. New York Transit Authority adopted a rule that no one in a methadone program could work as a subway motorman, or a bus driver, or the like. This rule had (arguably) a disparate impact: 63 percent of all New Yorkers in public methadone programs were black or Hispanic. But the Transit Authority argued that the rule promoted public safety; and the courts refused to strike it down.[86]

In a case like *Griggs*, there is no substitute for disparate impact. It is the only way to get at hidden motives. But technically, "disparate impact" is not about hidden motives at all. The doctrine redefines "discrimination" to include actions which might be quite unconscious—policies which discriminate *in fact*, regardless of what the "discriminator" had in mind. There are dangers and drawbacks to such a doctrine; and these have been much discussed. These difficulties do not disappear as "disparate impact" moves into ADEA.

*Griggs*, of course, was a question of race. Disparate impact was soon applied to sex discrimination, too. And, in recent years, it has been extended to age.[87] Nothing in ADEA explicitly calls for the doctrine, but no matter: the statutes which *Griggs* "interpreted" were equally silent. Arguably, there is basis for treating ADEA as a special case. ADEA specifically exempts actions based on "reasonable factors other than age." There is no such phrase for race and sex in the Civil Rights Act. At least one commentator thought the phrase should make a difference: an employer should be able "to base employment decisions on reasonable factors that may accompany aging, so long as the decisions are not motivated by age bias."

What would this mean? One can test it by looking at *Geller* v. *Markham*, the case that applied "disparate impact" to ADEA. Defendant was a school board, desperately cutting its budget as the pool of tax dollars dried up. The board decided to hire only teachers with *less* than five years' experience. These were the cheapest teachers—and of course the youngest, too. Plaintiff was 55, an experienced teacher; she lost her job. The evidence was that 92.6 percent of the teachers over 40, but only 62 percent of the teachers under 40, had more than five years' experience. The teacher won her case.

Is this the right result? One observer, writing in a law review, thought not. *Griggs* struck down practices which "froze" the "status quo of prior discriminatory employment practices."[88] This rationale does not fit the age cases. After all, age and "ability" do correlate, unlike race and ability. And the correlation is not the result of "lifelong discrimination."

But the *Geller* case was not about ability; it was about cost. Older teachers are more expensive teachers. In a way, it is their fault that they cost more; salary goes up with years on the job. The disparate impact "actually was the result of the union contract that linked pay with experience." The older worker, then, was paying the price of a good contract. Mandatory retirement poses a similar social issue. The job market is brittle and rigid; it is organized along conventional lines of seniority. The law forces employers to be sensitive to the way rules and practices affect black workers and women. The *Geller* case forces them to become sensitive to age as well, to think twice about the effect of rules on age groups. This is all to the good, if you accept the goals of ADEA; whether it is worth the price is a more difficult question.

Disparate impact doctrine is only one of many wrinkles in the problem of proof in age cases. If plaintiff has no "smoking gun," disparate impact is his next best move—to show, statistically, that a company policy or rule falls heavily on older workers. Courts allow statistical evidence in age discrimination cases, as elsewhere. Statistics can show disparate impact, or some "pattern" of (unspoken) discrimination. If a company hires nobody, or almost nobody, over such and such an age, the statistical patterns are obviously relevant. Patterns are relevant even though plaintiff is an individual, not a class (or the government). Statistics cannot *prove* that the company did not hire Jane Jones because she was 50, but they certainly bear on the question.[89]

There is much case-law and a huge literature on the use of statistics, especially in race and sex cases.[90] The issues can be very technical. Trials turn into battles of statisticians. Each side rolls up its heavy artillery. The trial court makes "findings of fact"; on appeal, the higher court usually affirms these "findings," unless they seem totally out of line. This freezes into holy writ what the trial court "found." All this is standard and banal to a lawyer. But from the standpoint of social policy, it is a bit unsatisfying.

Without evidence of "patterns and practices," the law would be hard to enforce, except in very blatant cases. On the other hand, discrimination is a criminal act; it is, in theory at least, morally reprehensible. Should this label be pinned on a person—or company—because some arcane statistical test suggests deep-seated, perhaps unconscious, bias against people over 40? Should companies be forced to spend a fortune, and distort their personnel policies, because of "discrimination" so slight that only the most delicate seismographs can find it? If the label of discrimination is misused or overused, it might stimulate a backlash.

Is it sensible even to frame the issue in terms of "intent" to "discriminate"? It is a nice question, what (if anything) it means to say that United States Steel "intends" this or that. At one time, companies had explicit rules against hiring blacks or giving "male" jobs to women. Duke Power had been racist for years. Other companies refused to hire people over 40. This was not illegal before 1967, in most states. It was a form of "ageism"; but most people and firms did not know or care. The new law changed the situation. Explicit age rules had to go.

In the early stages of ADEA, statistics, and other evidence of patterns and practices, had to be a vital part of any serious enforcement effort. After the law was passed, companies would abandon any *explicit* rules that violated the statute. Workers and courts would still want to know whether "ageism" survived—underground, so to speak. In age cases, patterns may be especially important. Some companies or employers may not be aware of the extent of their prejudice, even after 1967. They may be more bigoted than they think—either out of ignorance or as an exercise in unconscious denial. ADEA is not as well known as the civil rights laws, there is less public pressure, and wrong attitudes are more subtle. Businesses have unexamined, or unexpressed, preferences for "young blood." Cases that use statistical patterns may spread the word, at least to big companies: they had better become sensitive to this issue. Personnel people will be told "For God's sake, hire some people over 40."

"Disparate impact" has in fact two meanings. It refers in the first place to evidence of real but hidden intent. But it can also refer to effects divorced from intent. This second form, where there is no "discriminatory intent," overt or covert, raises tough issues. Is it really good policy to outlaw all personnel practices which in fact produce lopsided effects? For example, would a veteran's preference be illegal, if (as is true) most veterans are men?[91] The Supreme Court has struggled with the problem in a number of cases (none on age as such). A complicated tissue of doctrine has emerged. It is clear that disparate impact alone is not enough, whatever the language of the cases. Just because a rule or practice does not fall evenly on old and young, male and female, black and white, does not mean it violates the law. Women lost the battle against the veteran's preference. But evidence of "disparate impact" often does help convince a court to grant relief; this means, in practice, a quota system of some sort, imposed on certain businesses, or certain lines of work. Socially and legally, is this a desirable result?

There is a conceptual problem here, a certain muddle in language and meaning, which pervades many discussions of age discrimination. The Age Discrimination Study can be used to illustrate the point. This is the report which Congress ordered when it passed ADA—a study of age discrimination in federally funded programs. The Commission on Civil Rights prepared the report and published it in 1979.[92]

First off, the commission had to define its terms. Its "tentative" definition of discrimination was as follows: "any act or failure to act, or any law or policy that adversely affects an individual on the basis of age" (p. 5). But this does not define "discrimination" at all; rather, it states something like the disparate impact doctrine. The commission went on to outline a "two-step process" in making "findings" of "unreasonable age discrimination." First it would measure disparate impact (for example, does the "age distribution of program beneficiaries" differ from "the age distribution of those eligible to benefit"?). Then it would decide if the "disparity" is "justifiable or not." This of course departs from the definition: it implies that some "discrimination" is "justified."

To answer its own questions, the commission carried out field studies. For example, it studied federally funded legal services programs. The commission found "substantial underservice to persons 65 or over" (p. 105). Between 13.6 and 25 percent of the people eligible for the program were "older persons"; but, in fact, the elderly made up 13.6 percent or more of the clients in only six projects out of eighty-two surveyed.

Why was this? Thomas Ehrlich, then president of the Legal Services Corporation, tried to explain: people who are old and poor have "transportation difficulties"; they tend to be "less aware" of programs and "do not understand how the programs can be helpful." The solution: "aggressive outreach efforts, such as making presentations in senior citizens centers and nursing homes" (p. 109).

Of course, the Legal Services Corporation *should* take these problems into account, if it wants to be more effective or useful to elderly clients. "Outreach" is a good idea. But is it "discrimination" *not* to use outreach? "Outreach" is in fact a kind of affirmative action—a special step taken, past the point of neutrality, to make up for lost time and lost ground. Does "ageism" require it or need it? The analogy with race falters here, and rather dramatically. There *are* some special programs for the elderly—housing, Social Security, and so on. These remain in effect and are quite significant. Affirmative action for blacks steps into a different world: a deadly void, a historical abyss.

In discrimination cases, there is some danger that the tail will wag the dog, that procedure will give birth to substance. The disparate impact doctrine began as a solution to problems of proof. This and other doctrines end up, in fact, as positive rules about hiring and firing. They end up, in a way, as fresh *duties* imposed on employers.

At some point, "patterns and practices" become controversial; and some people claim they may do more harm than good. Business, universities, government, and society in general begin to consider them nuisances. One special problem— alas, all too salient in hard times—has to do with "reductions in force" (mass firings) in companies and agencies forced to cut back because of falling sales or shrinking business. Older employees are usually more expensive than younger ones. When a company cuts back, it may prefer to get rid of employees it considers the most expensive, and who do not seem to be quite so easy to shift around in the company.[93] This was the problem in the *Geller* case. Is this age discrimination? It has an impact on older workers. Establishing a "pattern or practice" makes out a *prima facie* case.

Hiring decisions are decentralized in many companies. In *Marshall* v. *Goodyear Tire and Rubber Co.*,[94] a local store manager fired one employee, probably illegally. The employee sued, and Goodyear—an enormous company—faced the threat of an injunction, company-wide and nation-wide. It argued against the injunction: age discrimination (the company said) was against company policy. The incident in the case was local, isolated, and not the fault of management at all. An injunction would be far too harsh. The Circuit Court agreed. "ADEA . . . does not require centralized supervision of employment decisions."

But in a way it does. A company faces lawsuits, unless it makes sure correct policy is followed, all over its empire. In the *Goodyear* case, no one questioned the basic fact that Goodyear was liable. Companies are responsible for discrimination at every level, and it is not enough to enunciate "company policy" against bigotry. The company has to protect itself by adopting rules and procedures that ensure compliance down to the smallest unit. The result is further legalization—an increase in formality, in other words.

The point is brought home when a court complains that a company used "subjective" criteria in deciding whom to throw overboard when a division or plant closed down. The company's mistake was letting supervisors pick the people to be fired, without "any definite identifiable criteria based on quality or quantity of work or specific performances that were supported by some kind of record."[95] No wonder that a commentator on ADEA advises companies to use an "objective system" in cutting back on workers. But an "objective" system means a formal system, a system of rules; a system that builds up a written record to justify firing Ms. B or Mr. A.[96]

There is no doubt, then, that the law encourages formality, or (to put it less kindly) red tape. This is a consequence, too, of the use of the *McDonnell Douglas*[97] doctrine in age cases. The doctrine, which (like disparate impact) comes out of the race decisions, has to do with the steps an individual plaintiff has to take to set up a *prima facie* case for his lawsuit. The Court in *McDonnell Douglas* outlined four of these steps, for a case in which, let us say, the plaintiff tried to get a job and was turned down. He makes his *prima facie* case by showing that he belonged to a "racial minority"; that he was qualified for the job he applied for; that he was nonetheless rejected; and that the job stayed open and the employer kept taking applications, or hired somebody else.

Once a plaintiff makes out this preliminary case, it is up to the employer to show some "legitimate, nondiscriminatory reason" why plaintiff did not get the job. If the employer cannot show this, plaintiff will probably win. Federal courts in ADEA cases have basically accepted *McDonnell Douglas* and its guidelines.[98] Age, unlike race, is a continuous variable; and this requires a bit more leeway in applying the fourth step of the guidelines— for example, the employer might hire somebody within the "protected group," but younger than plaintiff. In other words, a 60-year-old can still make out a *prima-facie* case if the company hired a 45-year-old instead.[99]

Of course, discussion of tests, guidelines, burdens of proof, and the like hardly captures the realities of law or of life. The economy somehow has to function, workers have to be hired and fired; and lawyers have to advise their clients, on either side, even if the doctrines spun out by federal courts are fuzzy and intricate. The plain result is to reward employers with clear, careful, objective, personnel practices; and to disfavor subjective, personal decisions. In other words, it is dangerous to grant great discretion to hirers and firers; the better course is to insist on a full and careful "record" in employment decisions.

ADEA follows here in the footsteps of race and sex. Its importance has grown, in size and scope; exceptions have shriveled and the concept of "discrimination" has gotten larger, more gaseous, more diffuse. Expansion comes disguised, in part, in the form of rules of procedure and proof; but the effect on company behavior is apt to be the same.

*Legalization* depends on public consciousness of claims and a willingness to enforce them. In the *Goodyear* case, we suggested how formality followed, as a natural consequence, from the way ADEA has been interpreted in court. There is thus a crucial link between litigation and legalization. ADEA created *rights*. There is an increasing tendency to use them. Litigation is on the rise, even though the law stresses conciliation, and even though most complaints never get to court. Perhaps some fraction of employers is obstinate and unyielding; or some fraction of employees is fractious and demanding. In any event, court action is a kind of last resort, but an important one. The question is: for whom?

There are more and more reported cases on the books, though the numbers are still modest compared with other fields. One published study counted 232 cases up to February 1979, in the federal courts (trial and appeal courts alike).[100] I analyzed a more restricted subset: all cases of age discrimination which reached the federal circuit courts (that is, the intermediate-level federal courts) as of February 11, 1982. There were 190 such cases.

Congress probably expected that enforcement agencies would

bring most of the lawsuits, acting on behalf of the victims. Yet 153 of our 190 cases were brought by private plaintiffs. Most of these (137) were men; only 16 plaintiffs were women. Of course, there are more men than women in the job market, but the imbalance is still overwhelming. Exactly what causes it is hard to say. As we shall see, plaintiffs are disproportionately executives or professionals; men hold most of these jobs. Women may also prefer to use Title VII and base their claims on sex discrimination; this surely accounts for some of the imbalance.[101]

The 153 plaintiffs are not a random cross section of workers. Most of them seem to be white-collar workers or professionals. In slightly fewer than half the cases, plaintiff's occupation was not apparent from the case reports. A few blue-collar workers may be hidden among these cases. Still, blue-collar workers seem strikingly rare (about 10 percent). Among the plaintiffs can be found engineers, attorneys, teachers, sales managers, executives, and administrators. Office workers and office managers are well represented. In at least four cases, plaintiff was an airline pilot.

Most plaintiffs (100 out of 136 for which there were data) complained because they had lost their jobs. There were only a few complaints of failure to hire (11). Complaints about failure to promote are a bit more common (21) and seem to be becoming more popular (15 of the 21 were within the last year and a half covered by the study). Most cases, in other words, were cases in which the employment relationship had been broken off. In 25 of the 100 termination cases, plaintiff had not been fired but rather retired against his will.

For 130 of the cases, we know the employer's main defense. In 52 cases, about 40 percent of this group, the defense was essentially procedural; a procedural point was one of several defenses in a few additional cases. (The 1979 study, mentioned above, reports even more striking dominance of procedure. In that study, 176 out of 232 cases were decided on procedural issues; only 56 turned on matters of substance.)[102] One procedural defense was far and away the most common; in no fewer than 40 cases, defendant argued that plaintiff had failed to file timely notice of intent to sue with the relevant agency. In 50 cases, the employer simply denied the *fact* of discrimination: it claimed it had a legitimate reason (not age) for firing or failing to hire. BFOQ appeared rarely—it was the major defense in only 6 cases.

Defendants, on the whole, did slightly better than plaintiffs. Disposition is known for 146 cases. Defendants won half of these (73 cases). Plaintiffs won only 11 cases outright. (These were cases that affirmed a judgment for plaintiff.) In 62 cases, plaintiff won in the sense that the case was remanded. In these cases, the courts overturned judgments for defendant (or dismissals) won in the trial court.

Not all federal cases are reported. This is particularly true of trial court cases on the district court level. Reported cases, then, are always (or almost always) the tip of some sort of iceberg. That may be fine; after all, as we said, the bottom of an iceberg may be much like the top, that is, essentially ice. Reported cases, on the other hand, may or may not tell us much about unreported cases or about ordinary complaints against age discrimination. One thing we know: reported cases are cases that were not filtered out earlier, or settled, or conciliated. If plaintiff sues on his own, the chances are that EEOC did not consider the case meritorious. In the light of these facts, the success of plaintiffs may be, on the whole, rather remarkable.

The cases themselves, as reported, tend to be dry pieces of toast—exercises in arid proceduralism, or so it seems. But sometimes the underlying life situation is uncommonly revealing. In some cases, which are particularly interesting, the casual reader wonders whether "discrimination" is the issue at all. In *Simmons* v. *McGuffey* (1980),[103] Simmons, 51, was administrator of a nursing home. He was fired and replaced by a 34-year-old. Simmons had been the son-in-law of one of the owners. Then he got divorced. The board of directors voted not to renew his contract. Simmons lost his wife, his job—and the case.

Was Simmons really fired because of his age? Unlikely. Did he *think* he was? Also unlikely; but perhaps he himself was not sure. Did Goldman, plaintiff in a 1979 case, think age was his trouble at Sears, Roebuck and Co.? Goldman worked at the Sears store in Saugus, Massachusetts, in the department of "big-ticket" appliances. After a management change, he was dropped to the shoe department. Selling shoes was an ordeal for him, because of a back injury; later he got an even worse job in the electrical department. Goldman, who was Jewish, also threw in a complaint of religious discrimination, under Title VII.[104]

Even stranger cases wash up in the reports or in the newspapers. Lucine Amara, the opera singer, accused the

Metropolitan Opera Company of age discrimination. A contract dispute was raging. Ms. Amara was 54. She filed a complaint with the New York State Division of Human Rights. The Met objected. No "government agency" could tell it how to make "an artistic policy decision." Still, for whatever reason, early in 1981, the two sides smoothed things over, and Ms. Amara sang a role in *Un Ballo in Maschera*.[105]

The devil himself, so the saying goes, knows not the mind of man. Nobody can peek inside the head of these plaintiffs, nor can anyone tell whether the men who fired them were "ageists" or not. Job loss is a crushing blow, psychologically speaking; it hurts the soul as well as the pocketbook.[106] How many people are strong enough to face the possibility that they did a bad job, or were "over the hill," and that the firing was justified? It is only human to put the blame on somebody else. And employers often *are* unfair, in one way or another.

But unfairness is not against the law, at least not in so many words. Discrimination is. The cases suggest that litigants sometimes use the law as a weapon, to continue a battle or to shift blame for their problems, whether justified legally or not. Many plaintiffs are no doubt sincere in thinking their employer was discriminatory. Complaints of discrimination can also be used as bargaining chips—and rather cynically, if one chooses. The same is true, of course, of complaints about sex and race discrimination. The law has, to be sure, guaranteed plenty of bargaining chips to employers. Antidiscrimination laws produce a certain shift of power, from one side to the other.

## Enforcement of ADA

ADA is a more recent statute, and less is known about enforcement. Perhaps there is not much *to* know. Certainly there is little litigation—so far.[107] ADA, said one of the very few courts to touch the subject, creates "no private cause of action."[108] David Marlin studied complaints filed with the Federal Mediation and Conciliation Service.[109] Between November 1, 1979, and March 19, 1981, there were 83 complaints. Marlin analyzed all he could (78); 56 percent of these were related to education; most of these (32 out of 44) were complaints about school admissions—medical schools in particular, but also graduate psychology departments, nursing schools, and the like. There were scattered complaints in other areas—denial of food stamps or of access to a hot lunch program—and a few housing complaints. The pattern resembles the pattern in ADEA litigation in one regard: most complainants were middle class and up. Getting into medical school is not a problem for your average Jane or Joe.

## Public Law and Private Litigation: A Study in Contrasts

Arguably, the case law departs from one of the bases on which ADEA and ADA were supposed to rest. The laws were concerned with *patterns* of behavior. No one wanted to get rid of individual judgment—judgment about merit, for example. Merit has nothing to do with discrimination. Neither does taste. No one accuses a man or woman of "race discrimination" for choosing a husband or wife of the same race, or going for a stroll with other white (or black) people, or buying a ticket to a concert which fewer blacks (or whites) attend than random choice would predict.

What one worries about is closing the doors of opportunity. If *masses* of businesses refuse to hire 45-year-olds, then a social problem truly exists (at least for 45-year-olds). If a person spends thirty years in the service of some company, which then goes out of business, the worker should have an honest chance in the job market; no arbitrary rule should shut her out of all decent jobs. If a few companies had a special taste for young workers, balanced by a few with special tastes for the old, no one would care. It is only when a pattern develops, tilting in one direction, that people come to see a problem.

Discrimination is, as we have said, basically a concept of *mind*. It is not illegal to refuse to hire any particular black, woman, old person, native American, or whatever, provided you do it for an acceptable reason. Prejudice is an unacceptable reason; but other states of mind are not illegal. Nobody can read minds, of course. The best way to put teeth into laws against discrimination is to forget about secret intentions and look for patterns instead. To attack the social problem, enforcement agencies *must* follow this course; they must go after patterned behavior and spend less energy on individuals with grievances. It is more important to

49

force a huge company to drop rules against hiring 50-year-olds than to help an opera singer who was fired (she says) because of age.

Yet the individual case has value, too. It can be good publicity, as the Internal Revenue Service knows. The vivid example gets attention. Individual cases will predominate, too, for management and professional jobs. More important, our legal culture insists on individual rights. Enforcement must not be the monopoly of the agencies. After all, government may be sloppy or half-hearted; industry might co-opt the agencies; bureaucrats can easily ignore *people* in their passion for patterns. So the law gives individuals the right to complain on their own, if they fail to enlist the agency's help. This puts something of a premium on aggressiveness and opens the door to all sorts of claimants—some who have good claims, and some who do not; some who have a legitimate gripe, and some who are just plain nuisances, or paranoid, or seekers of revenge.

The problem of the older worker can be compared with a problem much discussed in recent years: "discrimination," in rental housing, against families with small children. Some cities and states now have statutes or ordinances outlawing the practice of refusing to rent to these families.[110] The California Supreme Court recently "interpreted" California's civil rights laws to cover the situation.[111] No one would seriously argue that there is a general prejudice against children, or even against parents—except in this regard. On the whole, people like small children. In principle, too, landlords are free to rent to whomever they please. If a landlord wants to rent only to adults, and if tenants want to live in child-free buildings, why interfere?

Many people find the question unanswerable, and recommend: hands off. Let the market decide. But the problem is one of patterned behavior. Nobody cares about isolated actions and isolated attitudes. Nor would anybody care if a handful of landlords chose to rent to whites only, or gentiles only, or people whose name began with R; or who refused to rent to redheads and CPAs. Such landlords would be mere curiosities. What becomes troublesome are patterns—patterns that aggregate, patterns that threaten to become pervasive. Discrimination against blacks was absolutely pervasive. And when more and more doors slam shut on families with children, when landlords *pervasively* rent to adults only—at this stage complaints against "discrimination" emerge, and a demand arises, whether justified or not, to do something under law.

The same is basically true for older workers, with regard to employment and, in particular, mandatory retirement. A social pattern has developed. It would not matter if one company, or just a few, refused to hire people over 40 or retired all its workers at 65. But there were common, even pervasive patterns. It is difficult to break these patterns, except through Draconian means—through law. It may be a bit unfortunate, perhaps, that the law gets a free ride from the passion and struggle over race discrimination; that it borrows tools, techniques, and remedies from civil rights laws. But legal developments, and social change, are not required to be logical and neat.

By granting "rights," and by labeling certain action as "unfair," the law creates opportunities for people who feel put upon, for this or that reason, not necessarily connected with ADEA or with "age discrimination." The formal law becomes an occasion, a tool—it reflects a current of social change, an eddy in the culture, invisible, subterranean, but with important impact on the law. What may seem illogical in the doctrine, or in the way the law is applied, makes better sense in the light of this underground current.

Consider, for example, the case of Betty J. Moses. Ms. Moses spent 22 years with the Falstaff Brewing Company. She worked as secretary to Joseph Griesedieck. Griesedieck was a big man at the company—assistant to the president, then president, then chairman of the board. Ms. Moses, one guesses, was a very competent worker. Presidents of big companies do not keep on a bad secretary, just out of sentiment. In 1972, Griesedieck retired. The company then fired Ms. Moses. When a high official retired, it was "company policy" to get rid of his secretary, too. This smacks a little of burning widows on a funeral pyre, but in any event, that was Falstaff's rule. Ms. Moses was 48 at the time.

She brought a lawsuit, claiming age discrimination. In the end, she lost the case. Her job had been eliminated, said the court, for "sound business reasons."[112] No doubt the court was basically right. There was no discrimination here, as the law defined it. Still, what Falstaff did seems terribly unfair. Twenty-two years down the drain, and why? There is no way of knowing what went on in Ms. Moses's mind; but one suspects a feeling of outrage, a violent sense of injustice. These feelings led her to search for

51

some plausible way to fight back, some means to make Falstaff pay.

Judges live in the same society as litigants; they breathe the same air; they develop much the same inner feelings, the same sense of fairness or injustice. They decide close questions, consciously or unconsciously, under the guidance of this sense. ADEA is a specific text, addressed to specific situations. Judges can "interpret" its words quite broadly, but it is hard for them to stretch the text past certain limits of tolerance. Vague, open-ended phrases are much better, of course, than detailed, specific texts, in permitting social norms and feeling to be absorbed into the bloodstream of law. "Equal protection" and "due process" are perfect examples of this kind of text. In one sense, then, Betty Moses bet on the wrong legal horse. She picked an unsuitable text. But (at this stage of development) no tactic was likely to win.

Scholars who try to assess ADEA and ADA tend to assign a case like Betty Moses's to the cost side of the ledger. The case points to what some people might think is a flaw in the law. That is, Falstaff was "harassed" in a "groundless" case, where there was "really" no discrimination at all. Hence, it is wrong to allow such cases to be brought; they inflict needless cost on a business. But there are many kinds of "cost." Injustice, as society defines it, is also a cost, unless punished or resolved in some satisfying way.

I talked about Betty Moses's case as if it were some sort of side effect, or byproduct, of ADEA. But Betty Moses sued, perhaps, out of a sense of injustice; and arguably, this sense reflected a social norm that was in a way a *cause* of ADEA rather than an effect. Many pages back I remarked that ADEA had, on the whole, mysterious origins. Nobody lobbied and fought for it. It did not come out of any standard interest-group background. It seemed to shoot up out of the earth, rather suddenly, by way of analogy to race and sex. But race and sex laws were the product of concrete, definite, passionate movements. So, too, of laws for the benefit of religious minorities, veterans, the handicapped, even the so-called sexual minorities—yes, and the elderly themselves in other contexts, like Social Security benefits or questions of retirement.

This was a law passed "by analogy"; but what made the analogy convincing? Two points can be made here. First, civil rights law rested on one powerful proposition: in housing, in the job market, and in public places race and sex are illegitimate measuring sticks—and so are other "immutable" characteristics. The logic carries over to age; it is wrong to slam the door on men and women whose only failing is that they passed a certain inevitable line, whose crime is too many candles on their birthday cakes. The civil rights "rule" is to judge people for what they are, under the skin; not by the outer layer. Ethically, the heart of civil rights law is the concept of the individual—his worth, her dignity as such.

Of course, the life of the law has not been logic (except insofar as logic transmutes into ideology). The analogy with other forms of discrimination certainly helped ADEA; it could not have been decisive. I would suggest, a bit diffidently, another factor underlying ADEA, which speaks out from the Betty Moses case—not from the result, to be sure, but from the *claim itself*. This is a vague, half-formed notion of tenure: the notion that long-term relationships generate, or should generate, rights, even when these relationships are legally bounded by contract or have been, in the past, matters of unfettered discretion. There are other signs of this notion, popping up here and there in modern law. Can a well-behaved, responsible family be evicted from its home because the lease has expired and the landlord wants them out? Historically, the answer was yes. The landlord has the right to dispose of his property. But in modern times, this answer sticks in the craw. There are definite signs of legal change. In New Jersey, under a new statute, no landlord can evict a tenant —even a tenant whose lease has run out—without some sort of acceptable reason.[113]

Similarly, with regard to a job. It seems wrong to fire, for no good reason, a worker who has spent years and years with a single company. Unions, which have some say in the matter, protect "tenure" through seniority rules. Betty Moses had no such protection. A few cases in recent years have at least hinted at a change in the law. Courts have become more sympathetic to people like Betty Moses. There are signs of a brand new tort— firing an employee in bad faith.[114] In a few cases, courts have read into employment contracts an obligation to deal fairly and in good faith with employees. In one case, in 1977, the employee was 61, a salesman, fired after twenty years of toiling away for National Cash Register. He won the lawsuit.[115]

These are scattered holdings—straws in the wind. And, of course, there is no *direct* connection with ADEA. ADEA, indeed, was concerned much more with *hiring* than with firing. But Congress was probably responding, however unconsciously, to its sense of what is right, what is fair, for this time, place, and society and so, too, of the courts, agencies, and litigants who work with or respond to ADEA. In the passage of ADEA, and in its subsequent history, the sense of right has been a powerful motor force—especially since nobody argued the other side. The normative climate of the 1960s, or the 1980s, is not the normative climate of the 1880s. Ultimately, the source of all law is normative climate.

The normative climate is probably also important in understanding how the Betty Moses case came to court. It was (in part at least) the reason why she *thought* she had a claim. Legally, she turned out to be wrong, at least as far as ADEA is concerned. But many age discrimination cases—some brought successfully—are forms of the Betty Moses case with a slight twist of the facts, or in one disguise or another.

Take, for example, one of the most notable ADEA cases to date, *Cancellier* v. *Federated Department Stores*, the I. Magnin case. I. Magnin, a well-known chain of clothing stores, fired three employees, all in their early 50s, from middle-management positions in San Francisco. Philip D. Cancellier had been Vice-President–Stores/Operations; he earned $70,000 a year, was 51 years old, and had been with I. Magnin for 25 years. John W. Costello was Division Merchandise Manager–Accessories. He made $45,000 a year and had 17 years of service. He, too, was 51. Zelma Smith Ritter was a buyer; she was 52, had 18 years of service, and made $35,000. They brought suit in federal court, asking for back pay, reinstatement in their jobs, and liquidated damages; they also wanted the court to enjoin Magnin's from any further age discrimination. The case was hard-fought. The trial lasted six weeks. At the end, plaintiffs won a smashing victory: though they did not get back their jobs, a jury awarded damages of $1.9 million dollars. The Ninth Circuit affirmed this verdict.[116]

Most people probably find the decision quite satisfying, at least on the emotional level. Legally speaking, plaintiffs had a fairly good case. William Hughes, vice president of personnel and an "avid notetaker" (he probably lived to regret it), met in January 1978 with Magnin's president and other executives. They discussed Cancellier's future with the company. The notes say: "dead end here . . . Age 50. Maximum potential!" Two days later, Cancellier was told to take a demotion, or go. He was replaced by a 33-year-old. The other two plaintiffs, Costello and Smith, were branded "not promotable"; their ages were mentioned at meetings which decided their fate. These notes and comments are damning evidence, under ADEA; they are virtually a "smoking gun."

There was more. Throughout the 1970s, Magnin's was apparently worried about the "youth market." The company wanted to attract "young customers." One divisional manager wrote a report calling for "new, younger-thinking people who can merchandise and sell in tune with the 70's." San Francisco had "too many superannuated salespeople." Another report noted that the median age of Magnin's executives was higher than the median at Federated Department Stores, the parent company. Magnin began a campaign to recruit "bright, young" managers, people who were "comers." To make room for comers, of course, there had to be goers, and plaintiffs played this role.

This evidence was bad enough under ADEA; but Magnin's behavior looked even worse in some regards. In 1976, Federated introduced a Supplementary Retirement Plan, for executives earning $30,000 a year or more. To qualify, an executive needed a certain number of years of service. The plan was unfunded; any executive who left, or was fired, simply lost his rights. Between 1976 and 1980, only three executives qualified. Plaintiffs, of course, were among those who lost their rights. The jury no doubt suspected that Magnin was playing a dirty game; that it was double-crossing its executives, by getting rid of them before they could qualify for pensions.

This is perhaps the key to the case, or at least to the staggering verdict. Magnin was not acting in a fair and just way. It had violated the law; but the size of the verdict, the publicity, the ardor of the plaintiffs: these are best explained in terms of a sense of outrage. If Magnin had let Cancellier, Costello, and Smith go after six months with the company, would the jury have felt the same way? It seems unlikely. The Magnin case is, in a way, a successful version of Betty Moses's case. At the base may be a developing concept of tenure, spreading through society, in a ragged, incoherent, inconsistent way; and hooking on to ADEA for support.

I have so far discussed some aspects of the evolution of age discrimination law and speculated on social attitudes driving this development. This section will add some comments, by way of general assessment, about the impact and meaning of this novel field of law.

One place to begin is with an elaborate and trenchant critique by Peter Schuck.[117] Schuck's subject was ADA, which has its own special bag of problems (it suffers, for example, from terminal vagueness). But his criticism goes beyond ADA and applies as well to ADEA and its state equivalents.

ADA, Schuck argues, was fundamentally misconceived. He points out, correctly, that it was the "offspring" of the civil rights acts. In ADA (like ADEA), Congress drew a "fundamental analogy" between race and age discrimination. The analogy, however, is profoundly misleading, in Schuck's view at least.

Schuck draws a line between two types of law in aid of minorities or other interest groups. One follows a "nondiscrimination model"; the other, an "allocative model." The first is, essentially, a command to be colorblind, or sex blind, or age blind, that is, not to use forbidden attributes in making decisions. The allocative model, on the other hand, is a command to "distribute resources or impose rules according to particular criteria." These criteria are geared "to the specific social problem or condition that the statute purports to address." A program to build housing for the elderly, or for the poor, would be "allocative" in Schuck's sense.

ADA, Schuck argues, is a mongrel, a hybrid. It contains a general proposition forbidding "age discrimination." This reflects the nondiscrimination model. The *exceptions* to ADA, on the other hand, assume "allocative choices." Congress, in other words, "fused the two models without even addressing the fundamental tensions between them." This created a certain "potential for mischief." Similar criticisms of course can be leveled at ADEA and the whole field of "age discrimination." The laws are all careful not to touch *benefit* programs for the elderly, or such social institutions as the seniority system. Nobody argues that ADEA makes seniority in the factory illegal; yet if anything has a "disparate impact," based on age, it is this aspect of personnel practice.

The "discrimination model" uses race discrimination as a crutch and a pattern (sex discrimination to a lesser degree). It invites us to look for fairly monstrous inequities. Nobody finds them. It is only a short step from this discovery to general disillusionment. Some people may conclude that ADEA, ADA, and their satellite statutes may not be needed after all. They might, conceivably, even do more harm than good.

Schuck's study of ADA ticks off problem after problem with the "discrimination model." He covers the legislative history in a devastating way. Speaker after speaker rose up to denounce ageism, to bear witness to the sufferings of the elderly; but when it came to facts and figures, ageism vanished in a puff of smoke. All that was left was the fact that some old people live miserable lives. But so do some young people and some of the middle-aged. Race discrimination was on everybody's mind, but as a historical comparison this was somewhat farfetched. People were not lynched, enslaved, or burned alive because of age. They were not denied the right to vote, hold office, practice law, or (if married) buy and sell land, as women once were. The problems of old people might be seen as in an entirely different category.

No one denies *some* degree of "ageism" in society, especially a society that worships youth. It is a question of degree. Very little seems to be known about age discrimination as such. Certainly, before ADEA, there was rampant prejudice in the job market against people over 40. There is also widespread *perception* of discrimination. In a Los Angeles study (1977), Patricia Kasschau reported that one out of eight whites, one out of seven Chicanos, and almost one out of four blacks "claimed to have been personally victimized by age discrimination in finding or staying on a job." The survey sample was made up of people 45 to 74 years old. Huge majorities (87 percent of whites and blacks; nearly 80 percent of the Chicanos) agreed that age discrimination was "common" in the country. [118]

But these perceptions are not backed up by hard evidence; and they may reflect a single problem (jobs) which could conceivably vanish as ADEA takes hold. Since there is little proof of harm from general "ageism," it is easy for Schuck and others to brush "ageism" off as a problem. There are age stereotypes, to be sure. But social life is full of stereotypes—against fat people, for example. Are age stereotyping and age discrimination pervasive enough, and harmful enough, to warrant some major effort against them? And if so, are ADEA and ADA the right way?

Schuck of course says no. Some people feel that federal policy fails to do enough for seniors, or protect their interests. But this is not because of "ageism"; it is merely because society "has chosen to allocate its resources in ways that do not adequately meet the needs of that group." The remedy is *program*. In other words, if the elderly live in slums, then "housing for the elderly" should be built; if they are hungry, they need nutrition programs. A general ban on "discrimination" accomplishes nothing.

The argument leaves some nagging doubts. Spokesmen for the elderly, of course, disagree. It may still be true today, despite ADEA, that people over 40 have a tough time getting jobs, though perhaps to a lesser degree. Many doors are still closed to older people—in employment, in government programs. Dr. Robert N. Butler, testifying before the U.S. Commission on Civil Rights (1977), claimed that old people face "painfulness . . . loneliness . . . stereotyping."[119] The medical profession, for example, had ignored the problems of older people. Yet Butler's testimony was not directed against age prejudice alone. It was also a plea for knowledge and understanding—and for specialized programs: "Older people need the benefit of an outreach program. . . . You can't wait and expect older people always to be able to attend the community mental health center. They might have severe physical limitations."[120]

One can agree that both ADEA and ADA make too much use of the "discrimination model." (ADA has even worse problems: its blanket prohibition of discrimination, against people of *any* age, makes little sense.) Critics may be right in everything they say; this does *not* mean the legal attack on ageism is pointless. Of course to say that there is a social problem does not excuse any glaring deficiencies in the statutes, which some people think they see; or condone the failure of Congress to think the question through; or forgive the inherent contradictions, the mixtures of models, and the other ills Schuck has documented. The question is: what do we gain by the statutes and what do we lose?

One place to start is with the social costs. To begin with, there are dollars spent by government agencies. More significant, no doubt, are costs imposed on business. ADEA gave the Secretary of Labor (and now EEOC) power to investigate and also to "require the keeping of records necessary or appropriate" for administering the act [sec. 7(a)]. The regulations order employers to record name, address, date of birth, occupation, and rate of pay for each employee and to keep these records three years. Companies must also keep elaborate personnel records—job applications; résumés; promotion, demotion, and transfer records; records about firing; test papers; results of physical examinations; advertisements; and so on. Other regulations order record-keeping by employment agencies and labor organizations [sec. 850.3–5]. The case-law, too, as was pointed out, pushes the employer toward more formalized personnel practices. All this, of course, is an expense, and probably not a trivial one. It also falls, no doubt, most heavily on smaller companies. The bigger companies are used to record-keeping. How much new expense comes from ADEA is hard to say.

Bigger companies do complain, however. James Northrup, in 1976, interviewed about fifty companies, all of them "large Fortune 500 concerns"; he asked them their experiences under ADEA. He collected and reported a number of horror stories. Some were about groundless complaints from disgruntled workers. A careless personnel officer can provoke an expensive, annoying incident through a mere slip of tongue or of pen. It can be deadly to speak or write words that express a company preference for young people. One company, according to Northrup, was "harassed" unfairly by California. The state sent someone sniffing about "for a pattern and practice of age discrimination in hiring," then recommended "a complete affirmative action program for employing people in the 40 to 65 age group."[121] This, the company felt, was outrageous.

Of course, such gripes are one-sided and self-serving, and in any event unsystematic. Bureaucratic excesses certainly occur—why should this area be an exception? There is a general problem of "regulatory unreasonableness,"[122] and it undoubtedly crops up here, too. ADEA is another step in *formalizing* labor relations. It is probably not a major step—federal labor law, unionization, and sheer bigness are the main sources of formalization. Bigness itself explains much of the red tape on the private side. General Motors cannot run its business the way a neighborhood body shop can.

There is no reason to assume—and it is not assumed—that plaintiffs are always right and companies always wrong. Many reported cases give off a distinct odor of groundlessness. Plenty of plaintiffs are cranks or fools. In 1980, an expert on older workers claimed that white male workers in their 50s used ADEA to "get theirs," in the same way (litigation) that "blacks, Chicanos and women all got theirs."[123] (Whether these groups actually "got theirs" is another question.)

But it is a good idea to distinguish between what is legally and what is socially groundless. Betty Moses's claim was legally groundless—almost "frivolous." But it was rooted, I believe, in a genuine social norm. When "groundless" claims win, as they sometimes do, there may be a gain in social justice, as most people in society perceive it. This is hard to assess, let alone measure in dollar terms. Costs, of course, are blatant and obvious, compared with *this* kind of gain.

What else is accomplished besides some shadowy increase in social justice, and an arguable one at that? What is the point of, say, rules forbidding a company to ask for "young people" in ads? Under ADEA, no employer, union, or employment agency may publish a job advertisement "indicating any preference, limitation, specification, or discrimination, based on age" [sec. 4(e)]. It is not hard to picture what a clear violation would look like; and such ads were common in the days before ADEA,[124] just as ads that mentioned race or sex were once very common.

Age of course is not an either-or proposition, like race or sex. It comes in all sorts of gradations. It also has many sly surrogates. There are borderline cases. The regulations tried to flesh out the bones. Ads were not to use terms and phrases like "age 25 to 35" (a clear violation), or for that matter words and phrases like "young," "boy," "girl," "college student," or "recent college graduate."[125]

Here is a perfect example of what seems like bureaucratic overkill. It is startling to learn that the law forbids ads that say "boys," "girls," or "recent college graduates." It is a relief to find that an application form is not *necessarily* illegal merely because it asks for age or date of birth; it is surprising the question even comes up. But the regulations do say that questions on applications about date of birth should be "closely scrutinized," to make sure nothing unlawful is going on.

The regulations surprised at least one district judge. In a New York case in 1973, he held the regulations "unreasonable." ADEA was intended to help people over 40, he said, not "prevent their grandchildren from ever getting started." Nothing in the act, he felt, authorized regulations which prohibited "employers from encouraging young persons . . . to turn from idleness to useful endeavor." (The ads in question, placed in the *New York Times*, used the naughty words "college students," "girls," and "boys.")[126]

Two years later, in the Fourth Circuit, the issue came up again, in an action against Approved Personnel Service, an employment agency. Defendant placed ads with such phrases as "Civil Engineer, sharp recent grad" or "High school grads . . . apply now." One ad asked for someone who could type 50 words a minute and "get along with other girls." The government pointed to other questionable ads: "Sales Trainee, degree, athletically inclined," "returning servicemen," and "Lumber Trainee—Bachelors degree and All-American type suits this opening to a 'T.' "[127] The government even drew up a list of "trigger words," which it wanted banned as per se violations of ADEA.

The court would not go that far. "Context" was important. There was nothing inherently wrong with "junior" (as in "junior" secretary); ads directed at "returning veterans" were also all right,[128] though "recent college grad" was troublesome. The lower court had come up with a "subtle distinction." In essence, it was this: an ad or notice directed to "recent grads" is acceptable, if the point is to "acquaint those individuals with defendant's services." This is not discrimination, since young people have less experience hunting jobs than their "elders" do. The same words would be unlawful "used in relation to a specific job." It was also wrong to use "girl" or "career girls" to "describe an acceptable applicant for a particular job opportunity." The circuit court approved of this line of thought.

Did Congress have rules of this sort in mind? Perhaps not. But nothing can turn on what Congress had in mind, since Congress is so many and such busy minds. ADEA was new. It called for new, unaccustomed behavior. Some businesses would resist, that is, they would want to carry on as they did before. The regulations could accept this strategy; or stretch the text, like canvas, to cover whatever holes a recalcitrant might discover.

The regulations on advertisements, and the *Approved Personnel* case, thus have a certain logic. They carry a message: the law is in a zone of moderate expansion. Old patterns of behavior must be smashed.

The policy is debatable, of course. Why be so strict about the language of ads? Can business live with these rules? It is disconcerting that an ad may be legal or illegal depending on "context." The distinctions may be far too subtle for folks who work for employment agencies, or for personnel departments. These are not trained lawyers. It seems wasteful for courts, or the government, to scrutinize ads one by one. This then is another area when costs are obvious. And the gains?

Perhaps the gains lie precisely in the fact that the rules startle people. It *is* discriminatory to advertise for young people, to shut the doors of medical schools to people over 30, to fire people because they no longer think young. It is even discriminatory (in a way) to recruit on college campuses. Why do institutions fall all over themselves looking for young people? Why does I. Magnin think it needs "fresh blood"? Because of attitudes and stereotypes about the nonyoung—attitudes which are either wrong or socially harmful (or both). ADEA was meant to make people stop and think: do these attitudes have any point? Why are you throwing these résumés—of people over 40—into the wastebasket? Why are you looking for "young men," "career girls," and the like? If enough people rethink their attitudes (assuming one agrees with the basic idea), the benefits might well be worth the cost. How to compute these benefits is a mystery. But this is equally true of other civil rights laws, and of social justice in general.

These last paragraphs have assumed that there is something called "ageism," and that it is a true prejudice or, in other words, irrational. Not everyone agrees. "Age" is not an inborn characteristic that sharply sets off group against group. It is, rather, a part of the life cycle. We all get old (if we live long enough), whereas we are born white or black, male or female; the matter is settled at birth, once and for all.[129] But where does this reasoning lead us? It is true that, for all of us, our time will come. Does this mean that people empathize more easily with old people than with other "minorities"? Not necessarily. Most white males a century ago were sure that blacks were racially inferior and that God and biology put women under men. These opinions are far from dead, but they are less prevalent than they used to be, one hopes. Most people (including some old people) think of old people, too, as inferior—weaker, less quick of mind, and so on. Since we all wear out in the end, these prejudices are plausible and persistent. "Negative stereotypes" abound; even the old come to accept them.[130] But the basis for these stereotypes is much weaker than most people think. The question is: how can the facts about age be gotten across in a meaningful way, to as large an audience as possible? There is no easy answer. Racism is taboo, and sexism may be following close behind. "Ageism" still has a long way to go. Jokes about old people are still acceptable in circles that would not dare make jokes about race.[131]

Old people are, generally speaking, objects of pity or derision. If you live long enough, people will consider you a freak, even when you act quite normally ("she's over 90, and she still does sit-ups"; "he's 85 and still goes to the office twice a week"). When somebody over 80 (say) rides a bicycle, starts piano lessons, goes to college, or in general behaves like an ordinary human being, he is thought to be at least unusual, and (alas, most likely) rather eccentric. These attitudes are slow to change.

There is, however, some sign that change is coming. Neugarten and Hagestad, writing in 1976, saw society moving in two quite opposite directions. On the one hand, "age segregation" was growing. "Bureaucracy" was "bringing with it the increasing use of chronological age in sorting and sifting people"; age was also becoming a significant factor in politics. But, on the other hand, society was getting accustomed to a blurring of age categories: "70-year-old students . . . 60-year-olds and 30-year-olds wearing the same clothing styles," and so on. *This* suggested a movement "in the direction of what might be called an age-irrelevant society."[132]

The "age-irrelevant" society is, of course, a long way off. For one thing, certain social criteria will have to change. Here one might take a hint from the black pride movement. For blacks, it was important to insist that "black is beautiful"; this meant rejecting standards set by whites and for whites. Blackness could hardly be "beautiful" (in all sorts of senses) if beauty meant looking as much like white people as possible. Similarly, for old people to be "beautiful" or "strong" or whatever, they may have to evolve their own standards. If the standards are how fast you can run or how you look in a bathing suit, the old will come out in last place.[133]

In one regard, race, sex, and age prejudice *can* be compared. Attitudes on each of these start out, historically, heavily laden with biological mumbo jumbo. Scientists in the nineteenth century, and even later, gathered "evidence"—now totally discredited[134]—to prove that blacks were inferior to whites. (One natural history, published in 1883, claimed that the "Ethiopian or Negro race" was "unendowed with mental faculties or moral perceptions"; all "civilized" nations were Caucasian.[135]) Most people think of race as a biological category. Actually, this is far from clear-cut. There are biological differences between races, but they are trivial. There is no *biological* reason why society should emphasize skin color and related physical traits, rather than height, hair color, or body shape. Race, as people use the term, is a social concept—as social as "class" or "nationality." The child of a black and a white is defined in America as black, not white. This is certainly not a *biological* definition.

Similarly, feminists have had to confront "evidence" that women are by birth unfit for male pursuits, and not meant to be equal in politics, arts, and business. Most men—and women?— firmly believed this. (Many men and some women still do.) The differences between men and women are certainly important, unlike inborn differences of race. But these differences have to do with sex and babies, not with whether women make good accountants, doctors—or prime ministers.

With the elderly, too, we start with a biological fact: many people slow down when they reach high old age. Eventually they stop living altogether—the ultimate BFOQ is staying alive. The task is to unpack biology from mythology. Old people are probably much more capable than society is willing to grant. And the aging process is extremely variable; some people are hale and hearty at 70; others have broken down or are downright dead. When stereotypes about race and sex began to weaken, unfair patterns and practices began to get weaker, too. This will have to happen for the elderly as well.

## Age Consciousness

ADEA and ADA bear on what scholars have called "age consciousness." "Age consciousness" means that a person treats age as a defining characteristic. Race and sex, two key precursors, are also crucial means of social identification. Consciousness of race (as socially defined) is a massive historical fact, deeply ingrained into the American mind. As for sex, it has always been a vital category; it has defined who we are ever since the dawn of man, or, if you will, the dawn of persons.

Of course, people in this society are also keenly aware of their age, and what it means to be 15, or 30, or 85. Some think that age consciousness is particularly strong in our period. Neal Cutler, for one, thinks that heightened consciousness of age is one of "the most dramatic contrasts" between today's elderly and the "generational cohorts" who will be "the elderly of tomorrow." Tomorrow's bunch, in other words, will have spent a long time living in a society that has been incorrigibly age-conscious.[136]

Do such laws as ADEA foster age consciousness? Writing age categories into *law* arguably moves people in this direction. Law crystallizes and formalizes lumpy or ghostly feelings, adrift in society; it hardens them into definite shapes; and it sets up machinery that people can use, to translate feelings into action. ADEA and allied laws may create a climate of age consciousness; race and sex laws presumably do the same for race and sex.

But there is also some reason to be skeptical. Civil rights laws show a curious duality. The laws foster black pride and feminist pride; yet, on the other hand, they aim to obliterate legal, political, and economic differences between black and white, man and woman. Age discrimination laws also point in two opposite directions—toward age consciousness, but also away from it. These two aspects correspond to the two strands of age legislation. The "gray lobby" wants more benefits. The elderly also want equal treatment. ADEA singles out a particular age group and ignores the others. This provides a special benefit to a single age group. ADA, if it means anything at all (a good question), is meant to make all ages equal before the law—a different strand, a different approach.

Common to both strands is a fresh approach to the life cycle. In the past, people looked at the life cycle as a kind of one-way conveyor belt. People were born, grew up, took on adult roles (marriage, jobs, parenting), kept these for a long time; then they got old, gave up jobs and family responsibilities, retired, puttered about, got sick, got sicker, died.

The conveyor belt, of course, is in part inescapable. Some of it is biological destiny—the dying part, most certainly—but the rest is simply social, though "simply" may be the wrong word. In this society, as in so many others, there are definite ideas about age-appropriate behavior. At one time, as was mentioned, it looked eccentric or absurd for a person of 45 to go to school, for a 75-year-old to take piano lessons, for an 80-year-old to ride a bicycle or study French. For many people, such attitudes still hold. The laws on age discrimination are opposed to this idea. The ticking of the clock should not lock us into certain roles, should not doom us to one fate. The one-way conveyor belt is the wrong image; the life cycle is more "fluid" now. There are more second chances, third chances, more open doors—doors open to people of all races, of both sexes, and to consenting and willing adults of all ages. This was the point that Neugarten and Hagestad made.

Obviously, the redefinition of the life cycle is related to other social changes—the divorce wave, for example, which splits families apart and regroups them. Second marriages are in a way like second careers: a fresh start. Acceptance of divorce and remarriage is acceptance of fresh starts, at whatever age. Ultimately, the fluid life cycle depends on still larger, vaguer currents in society: mobility, subtle changes in child-rearing and parental authority, and so on.

In these life-cycle changes, law does not play a leading role. The real power lies elsewhere—in deep, global changes in social structure and social orderings, changes at a fundamental level of character and consciousness. Compared with these, the law seems rather limp. Yet legal structures play an ancillary role, after the fact as it were. Social change writes the script; legal actors help the drama work onstage. The impact of, say, a case like *Brown* v. *Board of Education* is, in fact, incalculable. What came before it was crucial; but the case set a process in motion, gave it legitimacy and strength. ADEA and ADA also come out of a social background. They result from, and reflect, the fluid life cycle. Once in operation, they legitimate the change, publicize it, harden it into rules backed by the power of law. *Legalization* is thus part of the process of change.

Not that these laws are necessarily the right vehicle or the best vehicle to advance, or smooth out, social change. They may be bad; or they may be flawed but as good as can be expected, for political reasons. Perhaps *any* law would pose problems. The statutes try to put muscle behind a subtle and difficult campaign. Enforcement agencies have to carry out the program; their staffs consist neither of geniuses nor of angels. The governing laws are vague in spots. They have to be fleshed out, interpreted, implemented. Workers in the field need guidance. Rules and regulations proliferate; courts spin out new doctrines.

Still, age law cannot be wrapped up in a net of rules. The point is to change people's minds, to alter culture and influence behavior. The *mechanism* is a blunt, dense tissue, enforced by ordinary people. The process, then, is far from perfect. Private litigation has a role to play. It gives the public a direct voice, an outlet; but it adds, of course, a layer of irrationalities; and there is never any guarantee that the "right" people sue.

Whether the campaign to alter minds will succeed is hard to say. Prejudice can be a powerful emotion. Discrimination originates in a frame of mind. Discriminatory *behavior* is another story. It may have one or more of three causes. First, it may be emotionally charged. Second, some discriminatory behavior is structural; third, some is based on ignorance. For these last two, *structural* change or *informational* investment may bring about important changes in behavior. There is prejudice against old people; but it is, on the whole, not as rooted in deeply irrational emotions as the prejudice against black people or against "women's liberation"; it is rather more structural and informational.

This conclusion gets a certain degree of support from an interesting little study. The subjects were some 300 MBA students in Pittsburgh, most of them men. They were shown lists, which described traits of a hypothetical employee. The lists were all the same, except for the age of the employee, which was 35, 50, 60, or 70, depending upon the list. Generally speaking, students did not react strongly to age differences (although the exceptions were always unfavorable to older workers); they showed no deep prejudices against the elderly. But when asked "Would you hire this person?" fewer than a quarter said yes for the 70-year-old, and only 38 percent said yes for the 60-year-old; 61 percent agreed to hire the 50-year-old, 67.6 percent the 35-year-old. Why was this so? The authors suggest "structural barriers (such as mandatory retirement) and concern as to whether or not the person will stay on the job." These considerations might convince managers that "older workers are more costly to hire."[137] It is this sort of discrimination that legal reform has the best chance of curing. In other words, structural change (an end to mandatory retirement) and better information about older workers could change people's minds, and perhaps their behavior. No amount of information can touch prejudice grounded in ideology or hate.

Structural discrimination can lead to disadvantages; but it is important to keep disadvantage distinct from discrimination. One remedy for disadvantage is advantage—benefits, in other words. If discrimination is the suspected source of disadvantage, a campaign against discrimination is in order, since curing discrimination might also cure disadvantage. It is tricky to give historical examples without stepping on somebody's toes; but at the risk of offending, one might timidly mention Mormons, Jews, Chinese, and Japanese. All had a rich history of discrimination in America. There was tremendous hatred—even violence—against the Chinese in California and the West in the late nineteenth century. The treatment of the Japanese in World War II is one of the most shameful episodes in American history. Discrimination is not dead, but it has lost much of its virulence with regard to these four groups. As discrimination ebbed, so did economic and political disadvantages. Blacks have had stickier, more persistent disadvantages. Long-term, deep-seated discrimination created long-term, deep-seated, stubborn disadvantage, which does not go away so easily. Hence the call for "affirmative" or "compensatory" action.

But what about the elderly? They form no caste or hereditary pariah group; membership in the class shifts constantly; everybody who survives will join the club. Is it enough, then, to get rid of discrimination? Or, contrariwise, is the only problem disadvantage, so that we can forget discrimination?

Some old people of course *are* disadvantaged. Some are not. A healthy 66-year-old with a good job, a house, and an income is not disadvantaged. The elderly poor may be severely disadvantaged. Some people would argue that the elderly are not disadvantaged as a class. The situation is, to be sure, subtler than that of blacks. There is, however, some structural discrimination; and this is the source of a certain amount of disadvantage. The heart of the problem has been job discrimination. This means, or might mean, that an antidiscrimination program, if successful, would end that disadvantage once and for all.

There is also a consistent demand for benefits—a demand that is generally successful. Benefits are genuinely popular. They have economic meaning beyond the client group. Social Security, for example, took the elderly out of the job market; old-age pensions helped millions of middle-aged people who had elderly parents to support. More recently, a real "gray lobby" has emerged, lending powerful support to the historical package of benefits, and to all other programs which the elderly see as theirs.

There is still another factor. The elderly may not be disadvantaged as a group; but when they stumble and fall, they fall very far, and irreversibly. Most old people are reasonably active and strong; when they are badly off, they are badly off indeed. To die slowly, miserably, in poverty and pain; to lose everything at the end: this is a recurrent social nightmare, and its strength helps run the benefit machine.

Age neutrality and benefits make an odd couple; but they are likely to stay joined for some time to come. Nobody seems to be bothered much by the mixture. Age neutrality coexists with big-ticket benefits, and with such trinkets as cheap movie tickets and reduced bus fares. What can possibly justify these? Nothing, perhaps. They may be like the (dying) custom of giving seats to women on the bus. They can be criticized as ways for society to work out feelings of guilt over the way seniors are treated; or as a way to infantilize old people, in the guise of respect, just as men infantilized women with protective attitudes and laws. But it is human nature to want to have things both ways, and the elderly enjoy their small comforts, one assumes.[138]

Petty benefits survive, along with important ones, partly because of the political strength of the organized elderly. ADEA did not begin as a program for the elderly, but it draws strength from them today. If the age ceiling is finally removed, ADEA will become for the first time a program that really *does* help the old as well as the middle-aged. This, however, is inseparable from the issue of forced retirement, which we take up now.

# Part II  Retirement: The End of a Road

## Background: The Road to Road's End

In 1981, the Chicago-Kent Law School, on the near north side of Chicago, sponsored a "National Conference on Constitutional and Legal Issues Relating to Age Discrimination and the Age Discrimination Act." Scholars "from the field of law and from the social sciences were present."[139] They read or listened to papers on the subject and took part in discussions, mostly about ADA, though also about ADEA.

Many of the scholars expressed doubts about these laws. Some dared to suggest that age discrimination might be, on the whole, a red herring. Others disagreed; they saw a real issue, and a real social problem. As usual, it was hard to build up the argument; that is, they were hard-pressed to make out the case that old people, whatever their difficulties, suffered from something that deserved to be called "discrimination."

There was one glaring exception, one situation where the experts agreed. This was forced or mandatory retirement—rules in companies, government agencies, and universities cutting the worker off, by flat rule, at a certain age. This, everyone felt, *was* age discrimination. The second part of this essay deals with this

73

one clear case. There is continuing debate about it, and a growing body of law.

Like age discrimination itself, retirement is essentially a modern issue. During most of our history, retirement, pro and con, did not sit high on the agenda. On a farm, retirement was not a matter of rules. Even in factories and mines, workers kept going until they dropped or dropped out. A lucky few had the money to quit when they wanted to. There was not much retirement, mandatory or otherwise.

In general, the law drew age lines sparingly. Usually, these were lines about being too young, not too old. No one could vote until 21 (later dropped to 18). Minors could not marry or make binding contracts. The "age of consent" was the border between fornication and rape; an underage woman had no power to say yes to sexual relations. At common law, this age was 10; many statutes in the late nineteenth and early twentieth centuries raised it to 16 or 18.[140] The Constitution (1787) set 35 as the minimum age for the President; for congressmen, the age was 25; for senators, 30. Nobody had yet said that people over 30 were not to be trusted.

Before this century, there were few overt rules that shut people out of work or functions because they had reached a certain age. Some states let people over 60 or 65 excuse themselves from jury service. In some states, those over 60 (or some other age) were completely disqualified. This was true in Alabama from 1807 until 1943; in Georgia from 1799 to 1875; in Illinois from 1827 to 1901; in Maine from 1821 to 1935 (for 70-year-olds); briefly in nineteenth-century Massachusetts; and for various periods in Mississippi, Montana, New Jersey, New Mexico, New York, South Dakota, Texas, Virginia, Washington, West Virginia, and Wyoming.[141] In a few states—New Jersey is one—there are still disqualification laws. No one over 75 can serve on a jury in New Jersey.[142] *Exemption* for overage jurors can be (feebly) defended, since it gives the elderly some choice; to disqualify them is inexcusable.

Mandatory retirement, too, first appeared in the public sector. The earliest laws, it seems, covered judges. A few examples occurred as early as the late eighteenth century.[143] The New York constitution of 1777 (art. 24) fixed 60 as the retirement age for certain judges. This clause, and its successor (art. 5, sec. 3, 1821 constitution), ended the judicial career of James Kent, who reacted or took revenge by writing his famous commentaries.[144] Businesses, apparently, did not force retirement on workers in the nineteenth century, although the historical record is a bit obscure. As late as the 1930s, according to David Fischer, most companies had no official policy on mandatory retirement. But many "operated under informal policies which had the same effect."[145]

The present system, then, does not have much of a history. Retirement was not, and could not be, an issue in the "good old days." Farmers "retired" when they chose; the owners of a textile mill could fire workers whenever they pleased. Without unions, seniority, pensions, or government regulations, there was no job security of any kind, for young and old alike.

The development of pension systems altered the situation. Private (company) plans began to appear in the late nineteenth century. According to one authority, the first such pension was put in effect by the Baltimore and Ohio Railroad in 1884. Other companies followed. The early plans were a far cry from their modern descendants. Employers were in total control. The plans never talked in terms of rights or entitlements; their language was the language of charity, as if everything sprang from the kind hearts of bosses. For example, Procter and Gamble's plan (1894) covered employees with at least seven years' service who were disabled by accident, sickness—or old age.[146] The pension board had authority to turn down any applicant or to discontinue any pension. The company could, if it wished, ask pensioners to do "such work as they can readily perform"; and could cancel the whole plan, with six months' notice.[147]

Westinghouse Air Brake established a plan in 1908 to provide "service pensions for faithful employees who after rendering long and efficient service may be retired by reason of age" (the quotation is from the 1914 version). The company guaranteed that the plan would remain solvent. But "no right or title" to the pension vested in any employee, except one who had actually retired. Company contributions were "voluntary." The board of directors had the right, at any time, to repeal the regulations "in respect to all persons who might thereafter have become entitled." Retirement was compulsory at 70. A worker could not collect a cent if he had been so foolish as to sue the company "for personal injury" except under workmen's compensation. An employee who left the company, "whether voluntarily or in

75

consequence of dismissal or discharge," also forfeited her rights. Mind you, this clause was *not* confined to workers fired for cause: "The Company reserves its right and privilege to discharge at any time any . . . employee, as the interests of the Company may in its judgment . . . require."[148]

Other pension schemes were similar, in broad outline, to the Westinghouse plan. Big companies apparently considered it worthwhile to set up these pension plans. For one thing, the plans bought loyalty and discouraged job turnover. Wells Fargo saw its plan (1916) as "an encouragement to continued employment with the company."[149] The plans also *discouraged* strikes, lawsuits, and other forms of "disloyalty."

Mandatory retirement was a feature of many though by no means all of these plans from the early twentieth century. According to a survey published in 1932, the most popular age for forced retirement was 70—overwhelmingly so in the railroad industry. In manufacturing, 70 was a popular age, though many companies fixed retirement at 65. Ages below 65 were extremely rare. Forced retirement was a key feature of these plans; it got rid of workers who became less valuable—it achieved "timely elimination of superannuated employees."[150]

In the history of pensions and pension law, the master trend leads away from grace and favor toward a system of entitlements, a system of rights. The first step was a shift in funding arrangements toward a group annuity system. Both workers and companies usually contributed to these plans, which were more "funded" and "vested" than the earlier ones. After World War II, stronger unions began to demand a funded system as part of their collective bargain. The United Mine Workers and the United Auto Workers were among the pioneers. UAW launched its drive in 1948; Ford agreed to a pension plan in September 1949. In 1950, Chrysler (after a strike) and General Motors also agreed to set up pension systems.[151]

*Inland Steel* (1948) was a landmark decision.[152] In this case, the Seventh Circuit held that a company *had* to bargain about pension and retirement plans, just as it *had* to bargain over wages and other conditions of work. The issue in *Inland Steel* was mandatory retirement. The company's pension plan forced workers out at 65. Inland Steel, like many other companies, relaxed its rule during World War II. Most young men were in uniform, and workers were hard to get. When the war was over, the company tried to get rid of over-age employees. The union filed a grievance and eventually went to court.

The newest stage in pension history began with the Employee Retirement Income Security Act (ERISA) of 1974. ERISA meant full funding and vesting; it said goodbye to all remnants of company paternalism. ERISA is a statute of breathtaking complexity; but at the heart of it is the rule that workers cannot forfeit their money, once it is paid to the plan. As years of service pile up, employer contributions become vested, too.[153]

There is a relationship, in a sense, between ERISA and the movement to get rid of mandatory retirement. ERISA weakened the connection between pension and retirement. Retirement is no longer necessarily part of a general bargain. The pension comes more and more to be considered a matter of right. The retirement issue is free-standing, compared with the past.[154] No worker would be willing to retire, after all, if retirement meant starving to death; anything that weakens the tie between a pension and *this particular* job weakens the social case for forced retirement.

But this puts us ahead of our story. Mandatory retirement was always, in the past, connected with pension plans. There was a sort of bargain: the worker exchanged his job for a monthly pension check. But who was behind forced retirement in the first place? Why did it show up in pension plans? Certainly older workers were not themselves responsible. Even if most people want to retire at 60, or 65, they have nothing to lose by keeping their options open. Ideally, they would like the right to a pension, at some age, leaving it up to them whether they took it, or kept on working, earning more for the pension perhaps, and retiring when the spirit moved them (or they sickened or died). There is every indication that this is what most workers want, or would want, if the choice were theirs.[155]

Most likely, however, plans were presented as packages: all or nothing. Mandatory retirement was dished up as the *price* of a pension. Unions who bargain represent most vigorously the interests of younger workers—heads of households, by and large. Unions, generally speaking, want to control or restrict the supply of labor. Also, unions tend to pursue a particular line of policy: steadily rising wages, higher and higher seniority, then dignified retirement at a reasonable age from what was perhaps after all a dull, bone-wearying, nasty job. If this meant compulsory retirement, so be it. Better that than (for example) letting people stay on at reduced wages. Of course, the union in *Inland Steel* opposed compulsory retirement; and generally unions, as we will see, professed strong policies *against* a mandatory rule. But mandatory retirement was, after all, what they conceded in the end. No doubt unions were sincere in arguing against forced retirement. Still, they used the jobs of older workers, consciously or not, as bargaining chips.

Government also moved toward compulsory retirement, for civil servants. In the early years of civil service, there were persistent demands for pensions and a retirement age. The system, wrote one observer in 1898, "will not be logically complete until Congress shall pass a retirement law providing annuities for superannuated and disabled employees." This would "crown" the whole "edifice of reform."[156] The crowning, however, took its time. In 1915, W. L. Stoddard was still complaining that "national efficiency and economy demand a civil service retirement system." Congress dragged its feet—"another mark of our inability as a nation to be businesslike."[157]

A Civil Service Retirement Act finally passed in 1920.[158] The retirement age was fixed at 70 for "all employees in the classified civil service of the United States." ("Mechanics, city and rural letter carriers, and post office clerks" retired at 65; "railway postal clerks" at 62.) At retirement age, employees were eligible for an "annuity," provided they had enough time in service. But they were also "automatically separated" from their jobs. A department head, for the good of the service, could keep on a "superannuated" worker, for a two-year term. Another two-year stay of execution was also possible.[159]

The 1920 act was not, as we have seen, a sudden eruption. William Graebner calls it the "product of twenty-five years of public discussion." There had been presidential commissions under Theodore Roosevelt, Taft, and Wilson, on joint questions of mandatory retirement and pensions for federal workers.[160] The debate, on the whole, was about pensions; mandatory retirement was a side issue. There was criticism because civil servants were already (some people thought) underworked and overpaid. There were only the merest traces of objection to the idea of forcing people to retire.

Parallel debates on pensions and retirement went on in the states. Some states passed fragmentary retirement and pension laws in the late nineteenth century. The big push came more recently.[161] Plans for policemen and firemen were among the earliest to be passed. Progressive reformers in the late nineteenth century criticized local governments as corrupt and inefficient. Their criticism extended to the use of "old and incapacitated" or "old and decrepit workers." Civil-service reform, coupled with pension plans, would force these people out.[162]

Other civil servants got special treatment in the laws—teachers and judges, for example. There was a great deal of piecemeal legislation for particular groups of employees, and particular towns, in the early twentieth century. Massachusetts was the first state to set up a general system for *all* its state employees (1911). Both state and workers contributed funds. A number of states in the East and Middle West adopted similar systems in the next decade.[163]

Retirement was an issue during the great depression. When millions of workers have no jobs, a kind of lifeboat mentality takes hold of society; the bitter question is, who will be rescued and who will be thrown into the sea? What usually happens is the opposite of the actual lifeboat code: women, children, and the old go overboard first; jobs are preserved for male heads of household. The others have to benefit in a derivative way. In any event, it was New Deal policy to make jobs, if possible, and to spread the work.[164] The Social Security law fixed 65 as the age for pensions; it discouraged older workers from staying on the job. A person at 65 could collect millions in dividends and still get her government check, but pumping gas or scrubbing floors for a pittance would be fatal.

Today this seems unfair; but it made sense in a wrecked economy. Massive unemployment had the country in shock. New Deal legislation had its parallels in the private sector. Compulsory retirement worked its way into contracts of collective bargaining. It would be hard to get it out.


## Retirement in the Courts: The Early Cases

Before the 1930s, retirement was not an issue in litigation. It came up, somewhat obliquely, in *Railroad Retirement Board* v. *Alton Railroad Co.* (1935).[165] This was one of the famous cases in which the Supreme Court tackled New Deal legislation and left it a shambles. It was a close case (5 to 4), but bad news for the administration. The statute in *Alton* set up a pension and retirement scheme for railroad workers. A worker was entitled to a pension at 65; from 65 to 70 he could stay on the job, if the company agreed; at 70 he *had* to retire. Common carriers subject to the ICC came under the act. The majority of the justices found the law unconstitutional. It violated the due process clause; it also went beyond Congress's power under the commerce clause.[166]

An issue of fact was at the heart of the decision: was there or was there not too much "superannuation" among railroad employees (meaning workers over 65)? Justice Roberts, for the majority, argued that such men were not necessarily "inefficient or incompetent." It was true that "seniority rules" meant that younger men were laid off first; as a result, "an undue proportion of older men" stayed in service. This was a tendency in the railroad industry, and the depression, of course, made things much worse.[167] This argument, however, did not change Justice Roberts's mind.

Chief Justice Hughes dissented; among other things he argued that "excessive superannuation" was at least a "debatable" issue; Congress was "entitled to form a legislative judgment." Congress could "compel the elimination of aged employees," if it wished to. Only the pension part of the law (and only certain aspects of that) was constitutionally dubious.[168] It was a "common judgment" that older workers ought to go. They should retire on pensions. Such a practice would be "fitting" for "large industrial enterprises," just as it was for "municipal undertakings." Policemen and firemen "normally continue so long as they are able to give service"; they are forced out, and properly, "when efficiency is impaired by age."[169]

Despite sharp disagreement on other points, both sides in *Alton* saw no *fundamental* objection to forced retirement. This was true of judges in the next generation, too. Courts that addressed the issue at all found no legal or constitutional impediment to forced retirement. The (few) cases in the 1950s brushed aside all attacks. In a Georgia case, plaintiff was a railroad conductor for the Georgia Southern and Florida Railway Company. Under a collective bargain of 1955, conductors had to retire at 70. The court found no discrimination "against any special class or minority." Did the contract favor younger men over older ones? No: the contract was perfectly fair, and affected everybody the same—though at a different time to be sure, "that is when each reaches 70."[170]

A federal case, *Goodin* v. *Clinchfield Railroad Co.*,[171] came to the same conclusion. In this railroad case, the collective bargain was amended in 1954 to bring in forced retirement at age 70. The facts of the case are revealing. Apparently, the issue had never come up before 1953. The members of the union, Blue Ridge Lodge No. 816 of the Brotherhood of Railway Trainmen, discussed the proposal at union meetings and put it to a vote, over the protest of older workers. A "substantial majority" favored compulsory retirement; the union then so bargained with the railroad. The union won in court, too, and rather easily. Plaintiffs' arguments were in fact farfetched (there was talk about bills of attainder). The court found no unlawful discrimination, no deprivation of property without due process, and in short no claim.[172]

These were railroad cases; they came out of a declining industry. As in the depression decade, mandatory retirement looked like a job-saving or job-spreading device. Courts saw no "discrimination"; and they refused to see the elderly as an interest group, or as a group at all—being "superannuated" was a condition that faced all of us in the course of time. Plaintiffs in these cases were also in conflict with their unions. In the 1950s, collective bargaining agreements had begun to include provisions for retirement more and more often. Unions generally opposed forced retirement (according to one study, opposition was "virtually unanimous").[173] But though they were opposed in principle, they usually accepted retirement as the price of a pension. A few unions were downright in favor.[174]

In any event, the courts did not stand in the way. Case-law was still heavily colored by the battles of the New Deal years. There was a preference for group rights over individual rights, at least in labor cases. The legal philosophy of the New Deal and its judges leaned in that direction. In the face of great crisis, society must organize, must pull together. It cannot afford the luxury of individual cranks who want to stop the machinery, public or private. New Deal labor law vested great power in unions; it deliberately left the individual out. The felt need was for *collective* solutions to problems.[175]

In any event, retirement (forced or otherwise) became normal in the 1950s. At the turn of the century, more than two-thirds of the men over 65 were still part of the labor force; in 1955, 40 percent of them; in 1978, 20 percent.[176] No one is sure of the exact reasons for this striking trend. Better pensions were certainly a factor. The connection between pensions and retirement is obvious, of course. Plants without pension plans, according to a survey in 1961, tended not to have compulsory retirement; three quarters of the firm *with* pension plans did. Compulsory retirement increased (in the 1950s) "with the expansion of private pension coverage." Of the millions who retired, some were forced out. How many, is difficult to figure. Estimates vary fantastically—from more than half to only a few percent.[177] Some studies claim that the majority of newly retired workers do not go willingly down this road.[178] On the other hand, other researchers present quite different findings: workers *do* want to retire, at 65 and earlier, and by huge majorities.[179]

Older workers, historically, did not make much of a fuss about forced retirement; that much is true. A study of retirement procedures, published in 1952, claimed that compulsory retirement at 65 was accepted "without complaint," if pensions were "adequate" and applied consistently.[180] But the same report also mentions that one company (not identified) asked 250 retired employees whether they were "glad to retire"; 147 answered no. The personnel officer of another company was "convinced that most employees do not want to retire at age 65."[181] The usual explanation for this attitude is that employees are afraid to be old and poor; they would rather work than scrimp. No doubt this is true. But there must be many workers who want to work, even though they would not scrimp at all. A lot seems to depend on the way the question is phrased. Probably many workers are unsure themselves why they retire. This could be true of those who had worked for years, under the impression that 65 meant the end. But the total, in absolute numbers, of men and women forced to retire, regardless of percentage, has to be great. In front of millions of workers stood this high, blank wall of refusal: retirement at age 65.

## Modern Times

ADEA was enacted in 1967. The text said nothing explicitly about mandatory retirement. Initially, ADEA laid down the rule that age discrimination was wicked and wrong, except for people over 65 (later 70)—and under 40, for that matter. The basic idea, as we saw, was to prevent discrimination against the middle-aged. This the act did; it fixed its upper limit at 65, precisely because Congress did not intend to wipe out retirement; 65 was the "normal" age for retirement. Most workers were not touched. Arguably the law did affect retirement plans, for firms that fixed the retirement age at less than 65. And, if Congress decided to forbid forced retirement under 70, it could do so simply by raising the legal "ceiling." In the event, that is exactly what happened.

The impact on jobs that called for retirement at younger than 65 depended on how one read a sentence in section 4(e) of the statute. The text was murky, to say the least. Employers did not violate the act merely by observing the "terms of a bona fide seniority system or any bona fide employee benefit plan such as a retirement, pension, or insurance plan," provided the plan was not a "subterfuge" to evade ADEA.

There were two ways to read the sentence. Under one reading, an employer could, in fact, fix 60 as a retirement age, so long as the plan was "bona fide," an obscure but weak condition. The other reading was that the proviso was not concerned (essentially) with mandatory retirement. It simply meant that an employer who hired older workers did not necessarily violate ADEA if he provided these workers with fewer or different retirement benefits, seniority rights, or whatever. That is, an employer could hire a 60-year-old, without the same package of obligations that hiring a younger worker might entail. But this would *not* mean that the company could, under a pension plan, force a worker out at 60. This reading made a bit more sense in terms of legislative history, though perhaps a bit less in terms of the English language.

Which reading was law? Federal courts reached conflicting results. The Supreme Court took up the issue in 1977, in *United Airlines, Inc. v. McMann*.[182] McMann worked for the airline until 1973, when he reached 60 and had to retire. The retirement plan had been around since 1941, that is, long before ADEA. The Court of Appeals had to admit, of course, that the plan was bona fide "in the sense that it exists and pays benefits." But it still could be a "subterfuge," unless the company proved that early retirement had "some economic or business purpose other than arbitrary age discrimination." The Supreme Court, disagreeing, reversed. There was a difference between firing a worker (clearly covered by ADEA) and simply retiring him. The statute was not intended to smash "bona fide existing plans." And no retirement plan dating from 1941 could be a "subterfuge," to avoid a law passed twenty-six years later.[183]

But the dissent (Thurgood Marshall) also had a point. Under the majority holding, United was in a ridiculous situation. It could force workers out at 60, under its plan; but it could not refuse to *hire* a worker who was 62.[184] Marshall consoled himself with the thought that the "mischief" of the case would be "short-lived." Indeed, it was. An amendment to the section overturned the case and provided that no "seniority system" or "employee benefit plan" could "require" workers to retire at an age below the statutory ceiling. The amendment made it "absolutely clear" that no employer could force workers out, plan or no plan, before the statutory age.[185]

By 1977, mandatory retirement had become much more of an issue in the country. Even before *McMann*, a number of litigants had attacked forced retirement in the courts. Plaintiffs trotted out various constitutional theories; they drew on the rhetoric of civil rights cases. Quite a few of the plaintiffs were state or local employees: Joseph McIlvaine, a Pennsylvania state policeman; Elizabeth Lewis, a junior high school teacher in Tucson, Arizona; Vince Monroe Townsend, Jr., a deputy public defender of Los Angeles County; and, a bit surprisingly, Allen Aronstam and Mark Horican, two assistant judges from Vermont.[186] A few plaintiffs relied on ordinary state law, rather than the Constitution.[187] Three Kentucky teachers, for example, tried to knock out the retirement rule of the Central City School Board, which contradicted (so they said) the state's general school law.[188] All of these plaintiffs lost.

State courts were almost totally unsympathetic to the assault on retirement. In almost every case, the courts rejected the claims. I found 28 reported cases on the subject, up to 1981. In 27 of them, the plaintiffs went down to defeat. Nothing worked: no doctrine, statute, or constitutional provision. The sole clear exception was a case from Hawaii. It was brought by an English professor at Hilo College who had been forced out at age 65.[189] Age, said the court, was an "inherently invidious" category. The university's policy was "totally arbitrary" and unrelated to any "legitimate state interest."[190] But the general run of cases was relentlessly negative—so much so that one law review writer, in 1975, came to the gloomy conclusion that the courts were hopeless on this subject; a "solution" would come, if at all, through "private or legislative action."[191]

The question reached the Supreme Court, somewhat indirectly, in 1976. *Massachusetts Board of Retirement* v. *Murgia*[192] was probably not a good case for testing forced retirement. Robert Murgia was a policeman; and police retirement has been something of a sacred cow, like the retirement of airline pilots. In Massachusetts, policemen were required to take "comprehensive physical examinations." Once past their awful 40th birthday, they faced even more rigorous tests each year, including an electrocardiogram and "tests for gastrointestinal bleeding." Finally, at age 50, policemen were through. This was of course far below the age ceiling under ADEA. But ADEA was not at issue. At the time, the act did not cover public employees. Murgia's argument, then, had to come from elsewhere; he relied on the Fourteenth Amendment ("equal protection"), that ever-bubbling fountain of doctrine.

Legally speaking, it was crucial to decide what "test" the Massachusetts rule had to pass. If age was a "suspect classification," like race, the statute faced a very tough test ("strict scrutiny").[193] Statutes that draw a line using the "suspect classification" almost never pass the test. On the other hand, if age is not "suspect," there are milder tests, which a statute passes if it has any rational basis at all. This statute passed with flying colors (and no gastrointestinal bleeding). The Court ruled against Murgia, in a brief unsigned opinion; Thurgood Marshall wrote the only dissent.[194] Physical ability, said the Court, *does* decline with age. Massachusetts removed from service "those whose fitness for uniformed work presumptively has diminished." This result was "rationally related" to the objective of the law, which was itself quite reasonable. Thus the statute did not violate Murgia's rights.

The only other relevant case at the Supreme Court level, so far, has been *Vance* v. *Bradley* (1979).[195] This decision upheld mandatory retirement at 60 for foreign service officers. The issue was once again the Fourteenth Amendment. Was there some rational basis for the line drawn between foreign service workers, who had to retire at 60, and other civil servants, who did not?

The Court said yes, deferring to congressional judgment. But the only "rational basis" for the decision was as flimsy as a house of cards. There was loose talk about "extended overseas duty under difficult and often hazardous conditions"; about "wear and tear on members of the corps," which could become so great that only "younger persons" should fill such posts. Was the court thinking of cocktail parties in Brussels? This is probably more typical of overseas duty than rough conditions in the handful of hazardous posts. The arguments in *Vance* were truly thin; and the case makes sense only if you think (as many do) that courts should bend over backward to avoid undoing decisions of Congress and the Executive Branch.[196]

## *The Next Wave: Statutory Attacks on Forced Retirement*

In the United States, when an interest group gets nowhere with the legislature, it turns to the courts. Similarly, when courts "fail," one can always try the legislature. This is what happened, after the assault on retirement lost decisively in court.

Results so far have been mixed. Congress has not gotten rid of mandatory retirement, despite the gray lobby and piles of hearings, studies, and reports.[197] Congress did raise the age limit under ADEA to 70. Effectively, this pushed forced retirement up to age 70—no small achievement. Congress also did away with mandatory retirement for its own civilian workers (except air traffic controllers, police and firemen, workers on the Alaska Railroad, and certain Canal Zone workers).[198] But advocates have not, so far, persuaded Congress to take the final, total step. The Reagan Administration, rather unexpectedly, came out in favor of abolition in 1982, but then apparently recanted.[199] It is possible the end will come. It has not come yet.

There has been a great deal of state activity, as well. By now, all but seven states have *some* provision barring age discrimination. (Three apply their statute solely to public employment.) Theoretically, of course, it would be possible to separate mandatory retirement and "discrimination"; but statutes tend to lump them together. Most statutes fix a ceiling age, as ADEA does; to retire workers younger than that age, by reason of age, thus becomes illegal.

Some of the state laws were relatively toothless, or were so construed. An Illinois statute (1975) trumpeted forth a "policy" against "bias" toward "workers over 45 years of age." There was a "right to employment . . . without discrimination because of age"; discrimination in hiring, promoting, and firing was "an unlawful employment practice." But the statute made violation a mere "petty offense," subject to a fine in the range of $50 to $100.[200] And in *Teale* v. *Sears, Roebuck and Co.* (1976), the Illinois Supreme Court refused to allow a *civil* action for damages.[201] The plaintiff, Teale, was fired at 56, had been with Sears for 27 years, rose to be "national buyer of audio accessories and repair parts," and was replaced (he said) by a younger person who did the same job. Sears told him his job had been eliminated. He wanted a million dollars in actual damages and another million in "punitive damages." He recovered nothing.

The tide, however, is running strongly in the direction of tougher laws. The Illinois law, for example, was repealed, and age discrimination is now dealt with as part of a comprehensive civil rights law, with teeth.[202] In addition, in a growing group of states, the age ceiling has been lifted altogether. In these states, there is no longer *any* retirement age. It is against the law to force anybody into retirement on grounds of age. These statutes are all quite recent and probably represent a trend. The most prominent state in this group, so far, is California.

The California law was passed in 1977 and went into effect at the beginning of 1978 for most employers.[203] The law applies to any firm with five or more workers. California ended forced retirement by the simple device of making it an "unlawful employment practice" to dismiss a worker over 40 because of age. There is no upper limit. A worker has the right to stay on past "normal retirement date" if he or she "indicates in writing a desire" to work and "can demonstrate the ability to do so." Employment lasts as long as the worker "demonstrates his ability to perform . . . adequately and the employer is satisfied with the quality of work performed."[204]

Alaska is another state with no upper age limit. Its statute makes it "unlawful" to discriminate, or refuse to hire, because of "age" (except where age distinctions are part of the "reasonable demands of the position"). The State Commission on Human Rights has enforcement power. Individuals can bring complaints to the commission. There is also provision for judicial review.[205] The act is very broad: any employer with "one or more" workers is covered; the only exceptions are social clubs, "fraternal, charitable, educational or religious associations or corporations," and people in "domestic service."[206]

New Jersey also forbids "age discrimination," but says nothing about any particular age. The first reported case, *Sprague* v. *Glassboro State College*,[207] was brought by one Archie L. Sprague, who wanted tenure at Glassboro State College. He was 26 years old. His department head recommended against tenure, referring to Sprague's "lack of experience"; besides, he had no doctorate. This gave Sprague, he thought, a legal leg to stand on. He dredged up a memorandum from the dean of administrative studies, which divided the faculty into three age groups, for purposes of tenure evaluation: young, middle-aged, and "over 55." The "young" (under 35) needed to complete their doctorate in order to get tenure. Those over 55 were "encouraged" to have a Ph.D., but because the "commitment of the college in granting tenure . . . is rather short," a "bachelor's degree and . . . a distinguished career" might do instead. The New Jersey Division of Civil Rights thought that Sprague had no case. The Superior Court agreed.

Another sweeping statute is the one in Maine. Maine passed a fair employment law in 1971. It covered age discrimination and had no upper age limit. Later amendments (1979) made it clear that the legislature meant exactly that: an "unequivocal intent" to prevent employers "from requiring employees to retire at a specified age." The law itself is quite broad: it applies to *any* employer. It does not, for example, exempt executives or college professors.[208] (University officials in California, lobbying feverishly, managed to get tenured professors exempted from the ban on forced retirement.)

Under Connecticut law it is an "unfair employment practice" to refuse to hire "because of . . . age" or to "discharge . . . or discriminate . . . in compensation or in terms, conditions or privileges of employment," also because of age.[209] The law contains exceptions: 70-year-old teachers or municipal workers, who are entitled to pension or retirement benefits under a state plan; people whose retirement benefits (exclusive of Social Security) are not less than $27,000; and those for whom age is a "bona fide occupational qualification" (specifically mentioning police and firemen). The influence of ADEA is obvious, as are the differences.

The Connecticut law, like many others, is part of a general ban on "discrimination." The word "age" was added to a list that included "race, color, religious creed, . . . sex, marital status, national origin, ancestry or physical disability." Mandatory retirement was thus, as usual, hooked onto age discrimination in general, and specifically linked to other evils (race prejudice, for example). Most of the statutes have the virtues and vices of the federal law. The purpose is praiseworthy, but the text is fairly brittle and unyielding.

These statutes are a great advance, from the point of view of people opposed to forced retirement. But they are far from perfect. They are not addressed to the social problems of older workers and show no sensitivity to the fluid life cycle. Some people might want to slow down, or work less, or differently, when they reach the "golden years." The law sets up no mechanism to fine-tune the labor system. It shows no sensitivity to problems of employers, either; and no hint of the fact that some older workers may be worth less (or *want* to be worth less) than younger ones.

Of course, flexible and humane job arrangements are not illegal under any theory, so long as they are not based on age. This may be the route that, in the end, will have to be taken— for the benefit of other groups, too, such as women (and men) with small children and all those not married completely to their jobs. Still, as of now, such arrangements are rare. And the age statutes, all in all, lack flexibility. They carry the brand or stamp of their origin. The attack on mandatory retirement grew out of the attack on "age discrimination." The "gray lobby" wanted to remove the age cap. It was not irrational to hitch one movement onto another, which was known, popular, had political sex appeal, invoked moral support, and had ethical overtones.

Most states, as of this writing (1984), still allow mandatory retirement at 70. There have been drives to enlist more states in the camp of California, Alaska, Connecticut, and Maine; some of these drives have been successful. There is a continuing campaign to get strong federal legislation. Politically and socially, the last word has not yet been spoken.

Retirement in general and mandatory retirement in particular do not have long histories, as we pointed out. At first blush, the rise of mandatory retirement seems almost paradoxical. American society in the nineteenth century was, for the most part, a society dominated by the young; an immigrant society, a mobile society, a society pushing out its boundaries. Particularly on the frontier, young men held the reins of power. There was nothing unusual about a 30-year-old governor or a state court justice equally young.

Talcott Parsons has made the point: a "frontier" society tends to be "technically oriented"; it values "technically specialized functions" which "can most readily be performed on high levels at the earlier ages." Age has more value in mature societies (no pun intended). ("Value" here does not mean respect, but the way concrete social slots are allocated.) As a society matures, it comes to value "organizational" skills (business executives, for example); experience becomes important, and this more or less means middle-aged people. At a still more mature stage, society gets concerned about what Parsons calls "interorganizational integration" and "fiduciary responsibilities." "Fiduciaries" are not actually part of the organizations they "integrate"; they perform, roughly, as "trustees." These are jobs for the old. He gives as examples judges and "religious functionaries."[210]

The idea is intriguing, but, if so, why should mandatory retirement suddenly appear in a "mature" society? One answer is that "integrative" jobs are rare, even in postindustrial America. There are few judges and bishops, compared with shoe salesmen, typists, and welders—or even business executives. In one regard, Parsons *is* right—"integrative" jobs do not as a rule require retirement. Supreme Court justices serve for life. Until quite recently, bishops in the Catholic church were not forced to retire, and the retirement age is fairly generous.

In another sense, it comes as no surprise that industrialization and modern times bring on retirement, voluntary and forced, in this and other societies. There is, as we said, no such thing as "retirement" in the traditional family or household. To be sure, in all societies, duties and rights get redefined with ages and stages of life; but *some* social role remains at every age. When a farmer gets older, in this country, he might find farm work becoming too arduous. He might then pass the farm on to the next generation, often keeping some kind of control until he dies. In this way, he avoids dependency and guarantees respect from his children. There are few King Lears in agricultural communities.

In factories and mines, on the other hand, the worker is landless and has no capital—at least none connected with his job. Artisans, farmers, small tradespeople, and professionals can, if they wish, "taper off." But in the factories or department stores, it is usually all or nothing. Retirement means total withdrawal. The retired miner or railroad worker has no work role at all. Retirement is "an either-or matter," as Parsons points out. Retirement completely cuts the knot that ties the employee to his job, except for the pension check, if there is one.[211]

For many workers, of course, this is just as well; the less they have to do with their job, and the sooner they can leave it, the better. The job is tough, dangerous, physically draining; or boring, thankless, routine. Do coal miners really want to keep on mining coal until they finally drop dead?[212] Some theorists argue that retirement is socially useful. It is better in all sorts of ways, if people gently slip away from their functions, as the years roll by.

This idea is a foundation stone of the so-called disengagement theory, which burst like a rocket into the sociology of aging in 1960. Cumming and Henry, who launched disengagement theory, argued that in every culture (and certainly in ours), society and the individual "prepare in advance for the ultimate disengagement of death by an inevitable, gradual, and mutually satisfying process of social disengagement prior to death." In other words, there is a double process going on: as we get old, we gradually let loose our grip on jobs, roles, relationships; meanwhile, these roles are letting go of us. Then the curtain falls.[213]

One way to look at retirement is as part of the disengagement process. But it is not the only way. Disengagement theory, as Cumming and Henry expounded it, has been savagely criticized and is now quite generally repudiated. The critics argued that "disengagement" is neither natural nor inevitable—it merely describes what *some* people undergo. It is, in short, a "variable," and it is influenced by many social factors. Many old people are or can be saved from disengagement through "activity," or by "feeling . . . useful and needed."[214] But while it lasted, disengagement theory gave at least some excuse, in the form of theory, for the institution of forced retirement. Indeed, disengagement theory, in its popular form, is an excuse to the elderly themselves: some accept the conventional stereotypes about old age and come to believe that retirement is good for them and society, and even that it is voluntary when in fact it is not.[215]

Retirement does not mean, historically, that society has committed itself to disengagement. Other economic and social processes explain retirement far better, whether they justify it or not. To begin with, many careers are based on what one might call a *balloon theory*. That is, careers are supposed to travel in one direction only: up. This is part of the very idea of a career. It is like blowing up a balloon. The balloon gets bigger and bigger and fatter and fatter; finally it bursts. On the job, salary goes up year by year; the worker gets more pay, more seniority, more pension rights, more benefits, more privileges; she may rise into higher and higher positions. There is no structured way to let the air out slowly and gently. At some point, then, the balloon simply pops. Forced retirement is one way this happens. (Another way, which I. Magnin chose, is to fire people when they reach "maximum potential" or are not "promotable." With blue-collar or unionized workers, seniority *plus* forced retirement has something of the same effect.)

In other words, the work force is paid *as if* age and experience have a value, though for most jobs experience adds little to what the job is worth after a certain point. A factory worker, secretary, sales clerk, or teacher with thirty years on the job is not much better (if at all) than the same person with ten. The skills may be the same, or slightly less. Moreover, the number of old people in society has been rising steadily. Hence they represent more of a threat to younger workers. There would be no problem if we could rely on most workers to die in their 50s. Coerced behavior—behavior subject to a rule—is a sign of social conflict; employment practices are no exception to this rule. There is an implicit battle here between young and old.

Society takes the balloon theory almost for granted. All sorts of institutions have grown up around it—tenure, civil service rules, the concept of seniority, and so on. Older workers are expensive workers. They are generally healthy and active; but they are not necessarily worth twice as much as younger workers. And some *may* slow down after 60 or 65 (or want to). There is no easy, graceful way to slide sideways or downhill. The balloon theory and the structures built up around it prevent this from happening. It is not hard to *think* of ways to let the air out slowly: part-time work, softer jobs at less pay, reassignments, gradual retirement. It requires no genius to spell out possibilities. Implementation is another story.

A white-collar variant of the balloon theory is the up-or-out system, found (for example) in the army, on university faculties, and in the foreign service. In an up-or-out system, employees *must* move on to a higher level, after a certain time "in grade." If the employee is passed over for promotion, he has to get out, even if the work he is doing, at his current level, is quite satisfactory. A young assistant professor *must* get tenure, or out she goes. Captains and majors "passed over" for promotion have to leave the service. Up-or-out systems usually have a fixed number of "slots" at different levels; the excuse for getting rid of people is that the system needs the right mix and number of people in each slot. Up-and-out often goes along with compulsory retirement, for obvious reasons.[216]

Mandatory retirement is closely connected to the balloon theory, and to a kind of up-or-out mentality in the structure of careers. The balloon theory also, and most definitely, stands in the way of attempts to solve the problem of older people who want to keep their jobs. Many people oppose "age discrimination" in general, but are reluctant to get rid of forced retirement. They worry about the expense of the older worker. Mandatory retirement would weaken, or disappear, in a hurry, without the balloon theory of careers and what it implies for the job market.


## The Problem of Cost

The problem of cost is crucial to any assessment of mandatory retirement. Certainly companies feel that way. Older workers do *cost* more than younger workers, on the whole. Can companies take this fact into account? It is not a violation of ADEA to let an over-40 worker go because of "reasonable factors other than age."[217] Is higher cost one of these "reasonable" factors? Specifically: a company faces hard times and falling sales. It decides to trim the work force. Mostly, older employees leave, and younger ones replace them. Younger workers have less seniority and earn less money. Has the company broken the law or not?

There are arguments on both sides. It is certainly possible to argue that cost of this kind is *not* a "reasonable factor other than age"; after all, cost is closely and deliberately tied to seniority, which in turn is connected to age. On the other hand, cost is *not* age; it is a different factor. The regulations take a moderate stand: in firing people, a company may not use, as a criterion, the fact that the "average cost of employing older workers as a group is higher than the average cost of employing younger workers as a group" [sec. 860.103(h)]. Cost is no excuse, then, for getting rid of workers with long years of service.

But in practice this principle is not easy to apply; and the facts of reported cases show how hard it is to decide whether cost or age or something else was the motive for firing a worker. This is particularly true of *individual* complaints under ADEA. In one blatant case, from the cutthroat world of the garment trade, Bertie Feitis, a 62-year-old designer, was fired three years away from pension time. The company, in a fast shuffle, dissolved, put itself together again as a new company, and hired two designers—aged 32 and 29.[218] It is hard not to react intuitively against the company and cheer when Bertie Feitis wins. But was this "age discrimination"? Did Larry Stein, villain of the piece, fire Ms. Feitis because she was 62 and expensive—or because she was expensive, period? Cost was probably also a factor in the I. Magnin case. To be sure, the company wanted "young blood." There was a suspicious tendency to fire executives on the brink of their pensions. But the company was genuinely worried about its place in the market. It was afraid its middle managers were not "cutting the mustard." An employer feels entitled to wonder whether "young blood," if not better than old blood, at least delivers more bang for the buck.

ADEA, one could argue, was not supposed to drive employers into bankruptcy for the sake of a principle. At least one court thought the act allowed employers "to consider employment costs," on a case-by-case basis, though they could not make a "general assessment" that older workers were too expensive. Presumably, this means that an employer, forced to cut staff, and faced with the choice of Smith (who is 65) versus Jones (who is 30), both equally good, can keep Jones because he is cheaper. But there cannot be a "rule" preferring cheap young workers; if Jones is not so good as Smith, then Smith is "really" cheaper, and Smith must be kept.[219]

Race and sex discrimination laws raise similar problems, especially in the light of seniority, which means that normal lay-off practice falls most heavily on new workers. Blacks and women fall disproportionately into this category; let us hope that this is a one-generation problem. The age cases are in one sense harder, and the problem may last longer. And it is a natural process to replace older workers with younger ones; when workers die or retire, younger workers step into their shoes. There is no such "natural" rule for race and sex. Involuntary retirement is an acute issue in hard times.[220] Companies have to lay off workers. Why not start with the ones who are "only" a few years from retirement? Many heated lawsuits come out of this context.

Here, too, the law seems excessively brittle. Companies face a genuine problem. A law review note (1979), after a careful and judicious discussion, recommended ways to soften the blows and do justice to all of the workers: job-sharing, "adjustment in the salary structure," reduction in hours for older workers.[221] This is easier said than done. The work structure as of now does not have this much "give"; unions, on the whole, are suspicious of or opposed to this sort of flexibility; management does not think in these terms. Such programs, too, would probably cost more to run than a simple blanket rule.

ADEA guarantees equality for older workers, not just the right to hang onto a job. Arguably, it would infringe the act to force older workers to give up privileges as the price for keeping their jobs. Logically, and legally, there is an argument for this position. (But perhaps not a good argument: surely ADEA does not force an employer to pay people more than they are worth.) Socially, the argument is nonsense: it is having your cake and eating it, too. At some point, the costs and privileges of seniority may become luxuries society cannot really afford.

Hard cases are supposed to make bad law. Hard here does not mean technically difficult; it means that the "right" side morally seems like the "wrong" side legally. Cost cases seem hard in both senses. The cases that present patterns of mass layoffs are technically hard and are the more important. They pose the question of how to spread the pain in hard times. Cases of individuals are hard in the other sense. How can anybody know whether a designer was fired because of her age or because she was expensive? Does the firer always know? And why should it matter? If the firing seems wrong, should the issue turn on whether or not it can be squeezed into a category called "age discrimination"? Many people seem to feel the need for a broader principle: protection against unjust termination of a favorable legal status. The law seems to be edging, slowly, in this general direction.

## Costs and Benefits of Forced Retirement

Meanwhile, as of now (1984), mandatory retirement lives on in most states, though in a weakened form. It has been eliminated in the federal civil service, in California, and in a growing number of states. The issue has been debated for some years now. What is there to be said about the pluses and minuses of forced retirement, or of the opposite principle, as it exists, for example, in California?

There is, for one thing, an economic argument. Edward P. Lazear claims that something like the balloon system, coupled with mandatory retirement, is "optimal" for companies and workers alike. Young workers get paid less than the value of their marginal product; older workers get more. A time comes when the firm will be "no longer willing to pay the worker his current wage." That is the time when the worker gets forced out. The system, however, is on the whole economically efficient; and the mandatory aspect is "illusory"; in effect, worker and employer have agreed on it in advance. The "date of mandatory retirement is the social and private optimum date of retirement."[222]

This argument, whatever its merits, presupposes both the balloon theory and a long-term commitment by workers to a single employer or company. How realistic that is, is subject to question. The real problem with Lazear's argument is its assertion that forced retirement is really voluntary. But the "bargain" he describes between employer and worker is at best a metaphor. The argument is based on a general preference for private arrangements, a rejection of bureaucratic "meddling," and an exaltation of the free market. Business should do what it wants. The market chooses the best, most efficient ways of ordering labor arrangements. The "reasonable presumption" in a market economy is that "firms seek out the arrangements that best serve their needs," as another economist, Robert MacDonald, put it. An insurance company that needed "patient, conscientious workers" might actively recruit older workers; a "first-rate university," on the other hand, or a firm "with team incentives or machine-paced operations" will need to get rid of its seniors when they no longer meet efficiency needs.[223]

But there is no evidence, other than ideology, that might convince us this is true. The current system was not produced by an absolutely free market, but rather by a mixed and complex one. MacDonald argues that workers will gravitate toward firms that have the retirement system they "prefer," looking for arrangements that yield "the highest satisfaction." If you abolish mandatory retirement, you interfere with the right of people "to determine how they may best serve their own needs," and you "disrupt" bargains "made in good faith in the marketplace." But these arguments would of course support the abolition of race and sex laws as well, which prevent workers and employers from choosing all-white, all-male arrangements to suit their "taste."

Several more general arguments are often advanced in favor of forced retirement. One argument might be called "let's not make a scene." The argument is this: a mandatory rule is more decent and humane than case-by-case decisions. Old people do slip and have to be replaced; a rule-of-thumb is snappier, less embarrassing, and saves the ego. It is no shame to leave a job because you are 70 and are forced to go, like everybody else. But it is humiliating to be fired as a doddering fool. Many (crocodile?) tears are shed over the "distasteful" episodes that would take place. At the very least, older workers will have to undergo repeated tests of competence. At worst, they will be driven out in disgrace.

This is a popular argument. It was stressed, for example, in a Missouri case, *O'Neil* v. *Baine.* This case challenged the rule that Missouri judges must retire at 70. The court defended the rule; it avoided "tedious and often perplexing decisions," after "traumatic and often lengthy hearings about competence."[224] The court cited a "field study" on removal and retirement of Missouri judges.[225] But the study did not support the argument. Few Missouri judges left office because of disability. It was hard "to crank up a cumbersome formal public proceeding to terminate the service of a sick or senile judge";[226] force or persuasion was used only in *blatant* cases. And there were very few of these—hardly enough to justify the rule.

Undeniably, some old people—judges or whatever—lose their grip. To get rid of them is unpleasant. The judicial system no doubt harbors old fogies and worse. On the other hand, the system also *loses* when it forces out experienced judges. Justices of the Supreme Court serve for life. A few have stayed on too long (Stephen Field, in the late nineteenth century, was a well-known example).[227] But many judges, including Field, served with great distinction in their 70s and 80s, and Oliver Wendell Holmes, Jr., one of the greatest of the justices, retired just short of his 91st birthday. Would the country be better off if Brandeis, Holmes—or John Marshall—had been forced off the bench at 65 or so?

Another rather hackneyed argument is what might be called the "vampire" argument: organizations need "fresh blood" or "new ideas." Dead wood is old wood, and it must be gotten rid of. Old people have (and cling to) old ideas. Many people sincerely believe this, including university presidents, some judges, and perhaps the executives of I. Magnin.[228] It is hard to test this notion, which is for most people simply a prejudice. And even if (statistically) the notion is correct, it is no different from the argument that old people are weak and sick, which is true for some but not all, and is hardly good grounds for a general rule. Also, the argument goes too far: it would justify getting rid of the middle-aged as well.

Next is "no room in the ark," or the "shrinking pie." The economy is contracting; unless old people leave the job market (presumably they never retire on their own or die) the young will get crowded out. Or, as a judge put it, talking about teachers (judges did not have to retire), "There is a surplus . . . [which] will continue to grow in size. . . . With the lifting of compulsory retirement . . . those pursuing higher education will turn to other lines of endeavor with the result that when sheer physical or mental disability, or death, thins the ranks there will not be quantitative, and possibly qualitative, replacements."[229] The problem here is the ethics of the choice—why must it be *older* workers who are thrown to the wolves? The answer seems to be on grounds of fairness: you've had your chance, now get out and let others have theirs. I find this less appealing as the years go on.

Some say, too, that no solution is needed because there is no problem; people *want* to retire. And, indeed, some studies confirm this. But this argument can be quickly disposed of. It is a question not so much of numbers but of choice. If most people want to retire, so much the better. The concern is about the others. And inflation, fear of loneliness, and many other factors might push the work force in the direction of rejecting retirement. There is undoubtedly a trend toward *earlier* retirement as of now; but the future is as usual quite uncertain. And earlier retirement is not necessarily the opposite of late retirement. Many people who retire early start new careers; they use their pensions as extra income.

As I pointed out earlier, there is enormous variation in estimates of the number of workers actually subject to forced retirement. Nobody questions, however, that *some* older workers want to keep their jobs. There are, and have been, companies with a policy against fixed retirement ages; they have no problem getting and keeping workers, and they are quite satisfied with their experience.[230] In the states that have gotten rid of mandatory retirement, experience will show who does and who does not want to stay. The choicer the job and the less physical drudgery, the more likely that workers will cling to their work in old age. At least this is a plausible hypothesis.

Lastly, there is, again, the problem of cost. Older workers cost more than younger workers. In some jobs, however, older workers may be better, more productive, more reliable. On the whole, too, older workers *need* less money than younger workers, especially younger workers with families. Society must begin to think new thoughts and carve out new arrangements. The balloon system stands in the way of creative job arrangements. Fresh ideas, one might add, are needed all up and down the world of work: for women with (or without) children, for men who want an active role in family life, for people who simply don't want to wrap their lives up totally in careers, for the handicapped, and so on.

In any event, mandatory retirement, as of now, has gasped its last in California (except for college professors and a handful of others) and a growing group of other states. How will the new system work out? It is too early to tell. Employers in California seem unconcerned; they have made only small adjustments. This is understandable. One common response is to give the old retirement age a new name ("normal" retirement age) and offer rewards to workers who retire at that age. Most workers, it is felt, will take their pensions and quit. Some employers claim that this is what happens.

But the situation, as always, may change. Higher paid workers may begin to stay on in greater numbers. Atlantic Richfield Company eliminated mandatory retirement on January 1, 1978; a vice president of the company reported that most workers wanted to retire (fewer than 10 percent stayed on after 65); but the *kind* of work was important. Fifty-five percent of those who stayed on were in professional, technical, or supervisory positions; only 45 percent were hourly workers or salaried clerical people, although these made up the vast majority of Richfield's work force.[231]

Another factor might be the employee's life situation. A single person (or widowed or divorced) working as a secretary or file clerk may value the human contacts, the feeling of worth, the sense of producing something that comes from going to the office every day. For millions of people, a job is more than just a way to earn one's bread. Work is the center of life; it gives structure, content, and meaning to life. It makes it worthwhile to get out of bed in the morning. Certainly, many people hate their jobs and would prefer to whittle wood, go camping, or spend the "golden years" among friends, grandchildren, or pet dogs. How many

101

people fall into each category is not easy to tell. And social preferences can change quite rapidly at times.

Companies could conceivably try to replace mandatory retirement with other arrangements. They might use tests of mental and physical ability to screen out the incompetent. Few employers so far seem to do this. A probe of employer behavior in California turned up very little of this sort of response (see Postscript II). Tests have been in bad odor since the *Griggs* case; and employers may feel disinclined to get burned without good reason. Here, too, time will tell. Or they might try more creative ways of dealing with a brittle work structure: part-time employment, sideways job shifts, more flexible pay scales, and so on. Here, too, one must wait and see what happens.

# Part III     *Legalization and Judicialization: Some Summary Words*

The development of law about age discrimination and mandatory retirement is a prime example of *legalization*. "Law" has been infused into situations where it was absent before. Labor law, in general, has been dramatically legalized since the last century. In the late nineteenth century, there was a burst of legislation on work conditions, job safety, terms of pay, the right to strike, and so on.[232] This was an age of industrial conflict, and the courts were drawn into the struggle. They took part rather eagerly. The labor injunction is essentially an invention of the late nineteenth century.[233] The New Deal of the 1930s expanded and federalized labor law greatly: wage and hour laws, regulation of union elections, fair labor standards law. In recent years, the field of employment discrimination has sprung up. Age discrimination is part of this field, and coming on fast. And, of course, "age discrimination" now goes beyond the job market. ADA, ECOA, and the various state laws extend the idea to other aspects of life.

The development of the law of pensions has been briefly mentioned. In many ways, this story runs parallel to the life course of other parts of labor law. If we look at the history from inside the legal system, taking account of legal factors only, we see a tremendous surge of "legalization." The story begins with a blank piece of paper: no legal rules about pensions at all. The private sector is in total control. Nothing is regulated. Today, there is pension *law* of staggering bulk. Giant systems of rules have come up out of nothing.

This picture is not false, but it can be misleading. "Legalization" is recent, yes; *formalization* not quite so new. ERISA did not come out of the blue. It was the climax of a history of private arrangements. The Westinghouse pension plan, however one-sided, was a giant step in formalizing informal (or unborn) arrangements. Next came collective bargains, less one-sided and considerably more formal. "Legalization" sometimes to be sure means creating formality out of nothing; at other times there is a *transfer* of formality—from private to public. A transfer of this sort, of course, is not inconsequential, either legally or socially.

The point is this: formalization often *precedes* legalization. What the law then "regulates" is a formalized relationship. Age discrimination law presupposes big businesses, big universities, big government; it presupposes job arrangements that are much more formal than the relationship between (say) a householder and a cleaning person, a farmer and a farmhand, a plumber and an apprentice. Modern life, with its impersonal, bureaucratic relationships, lays the groundwork for legalization.

A legalized society is a society that grants important rights to its citizens. To say that P has a "right," enforceable against Q, is to deny Q his possible claim of unbridled authority. If Q is an authority, or an institution, then P's right cuts down the social space within which Q might have had sole, absolute discretion. This "legalized" society of ours in fact teems and bristles with rights. Paradoxically, then, American society is, on the one hand, highly regulated; on the other hand, it lavishly grants bits of power and authority to private persons in the form of rights.

A "right" also implies a claim on the legal system. It is meaningless to talk about rights that nobody can enforce. Hence, a regime of rights blurs the distinction in the law between the domain of public concern and the sector given over to exclusive private control. If I have a "right" to a company pension, that means that I can call on the government to protect my right—I can complain to some agency; I can follow some procedures; I can (in the last analysis) sue. My rights of this sort are not psychologically different from rights against government—for example, rights to Social Security.[234] One kind of pension claim comes to look and feel like the others; and why not? They have similar legal character.

Social Security is a prime example of "social insurance," and social insurance is a prime feature of the modern welfare state. The people who receive the payments do not consider them charity. The pensions are "earned"; they are vested politically and psychologically, whatever the economic truth about the way they are funded. (In the case of Social Security, there has been a tremendous furor over funding and finances in the last few years; this great debate, and the constant warnings that the system might go bankrupt, may have impaired—just possibly—the feelings of certainty and "right" that had been so strong in the past.)

The sense of right is the very marrow of Social Security, and of social insurance generally. The welfare state provides entitlements, not charity and grace. But "earning" a pension (private or public) always includes some element of length of service. The key concept is a kind of tenure—this is what "vesting" requires. Legalization is the creation of enforceable rights; but these rights themselves only crystallize vaguer, more general norms abroad in society. The tenure principle, discussed here at various points, is one of these.

## Judicialization

The two areas of law discussed in this essay also show, in different degrees, the process of *judicialization* at work. This process takes two forms. As society legalizes, new types of dispute arise; matters become "legal" that were purely private before, or simply not thought of or known. Usually, some kind of administrative arrangement gets set up to settle these disputes; but American law almost always provides for backup or review in the courts. Judicialization can also refer to private or out-of-court settlement of disputes, but in ways that *imitate* courts. Many disputes are doubly judicialized, then. If a student who feels his teacher has graded him unfairly has the right to a university hearing, that is judicialization number one; and if she (or the school) can take the dispute to court later on, that is number two.

Legalization of the workplace produces new kinds of dispute, or makes old grievances the subject of new *rights*. If a company fires a woman because she is 55, it has violated ADEA, and she will have a remedy. She may go before an administrative agency, or eventually sue the company in court. It is also likely that a big company will have some inside mechanism to handle grievances; union and company may have agreed to set up grievance procedures. Often these more or less ape the behavior of courts. The same is true of administrative agencies. Their procedures may include many elements of "due process." Even when the proceedings are not *very* much like those of courts, they are likely to be more so than they were 30, 50, or 100 years ago.

There are of course striking differences between age discrimination law and the law relating to mandatory retirement. The first of these created a new "right," where there was nothing or almost nothing before; it made new categories; it established a "field." The laws against mandatory retirement are in one sense the opposite: they *abolish* a network of rules (most of them private) and substitute a new system, which calls for case-by-case decisions. Both are examples, however, of legalization.

Both also reflect wider social processes. Modern life is highly organized, institutional, complex, interdependent. There is bigness in government, industry, and labor. Bureaucracy and red tape in one kind of institution are linked to networks of rules in other institutions, generated, as it were, in self-defense.

It remains to ask *why* this reaction takes place. Of course there is no general answer. One point is worth mentioning. Many pages back, we referred to a trend, which Neugarten and Hagestad (among others) described. They picked up on two contrary streams of action. On the one hand, there were more age-related rules in industry and government; mandatory retirement is a perfect example. On the other hand, they saw the growth of age irrelevance, a fluid life course, in short, more freedom (and fewer "rules") in actual behavior.

Why do age-related rules spring up in a period of greater age irrelevance? One answer is simply this: there are more of *all* kinds of rules. A big company does not make rules for the sake of making rules. Companies are looking for efficiency; hard-and-fast rules make life simpler than if supervisors and foremen have to decide subjectively case by case. There is no hope of controlling a large organization except through rules. Only machines can mass-produce goods, stamping out preformed objects, from sheets of steel to little plastic doggies. Only machines can manufacture commodities cheaply, efficiently, and with control over quality. In social life, the "machine" that stamps out sheets of steel and plastic doggies is the hard-and-fast rule.

Rules are (or can be) efficient; but the stubborn fact is that people are not quite machines. They are all different, and each person in her own way struggles to make or keep a self in this complicated world. Modern culture also tends to exalt the individual—her uniqueness, worth, and dignity. Yet it surrounds that individual with a network of preformed rules. A lot of these rules are, of course, absolute necessities. It would be absurd to adjust the speed limit case by case, taking account of each situation, and the skill, situation, and personality of every driver.

Does this great swamp of rules suck down the soul of man into some sort of treacherous ooze? Yes and no. Modern life has opened up new zones of freedom. Consider, for example, the way the automobile creates new forms of freedom. It gives the common man fantastic mobility. At the same time, the automobile means rules, and lots of them: the speed limit; drivers' licenses and tests; parking restrictions; tort rules. Other rules enhance freedom of choice by *countering* the rules of private organizations and of other parts of government. Legalization, then, and its rules (about discrimination, for example) may be needed precisely because business necessity and administrative convenience conflict with norms about the nature and value of the individual. One should not dismiss legalization, then, as some new and dangerous trend; it should be understood as a reaction, perhaps a useful one, to the massive social facts of modern life.

In discrimination law, the main burden of enforcement falls to administrative agencies. But the individual is also a central figure, a prime bearer of rights and duties. The law hands him tickets, good for entry to agencies, courts, and local offices, and validated against (real or imagined) actions which impinge on a cluster of "rights."[235]

A system of "rights" has many virtues. People prefer "entitlements" to benefits that depend on somebody else's discretion. But rights do not enforce themselves. The squeaky wheel gets the oil.[236] Those with time, money, and skill make the most and best use of their rights. Rights are in theory "free," that is, you do not have to pay for free speech or access to a jury; but in practice the situation may be otherwise. The state does subsidize rights; but the subsidy may cover only part of the true cost. Many people (for example) cannot afford to hire good lawyers, who are needed for effective enforcement of rights. People may simply find it hard to take time off from work, if that is what is needed to get one's due by pestering the bureaucrats. Information, too, is a costly and badly distributed good; sheer ignorance keeps many people from cashing in on legitimate claims.

A system of individual rights can be expensive in other ways. Age discrimination laws mean paper work and fuss for businesses. A company may decide it will tolerate some degree of sloppiness in the work force rather than fire people who might raise a rumpus over "age discrimination." No business wants to be hit with lawsuits. If mandatory retirement is against the law, companies will let workers stay on, hoping that nothing terrible happens. They may sweeten the pot, trying to make retirement attractive. They feel they have to keep the conveyor belt from jamming up at one end. This, too, may impose extra (and "unnecessary") cost. The result of all these factors is a certain amount of inefficiency. There is, however, at least the *possibility* of rich, subtle benefits that counterbalance these costs. One such benefit is the chance that the laws express, however badly, norms with deep roots in society.

I turn now to another broad question—the dynamic relationship between legal and social forces. Age discrimination and mandatory retirement, of course, are only two instances out of an indefinite many that show this relationship. They are, however, suggestive and significant instances.

"Law" clearly emerges from a social context. As it does, it takes the form of orders, rules, or commands, which get translated into official behavior. Official behavior in turn has an impact or effect on people in society, who obey or disobey, or use or abuse these orders, rights, duties, messages, and privileges. People's behavior (as well as attitudes and values) becomes in turn part of the social context, the matrix out of which new legal acts emerge. And so it goes.[237]

This kind of formulation is so general that no one could disagree. When it comes down to brass tacks, consensus vanishes. There is, for example, the question of the *autonomy* of the legal system. Law is the middle term of the basic equation. Social facts create "law," which then affects society. Does "law" do anything more than *reflect* outside forces? Is it only a conduit, a bridge? Does it have "a life of its own"? Does it develop autonomously, according to its own inner logic, at least somewhat independent of the other social systems?[238]

Obviously, there is no yes or no answer; no global, general answer, for all fields, periods, societies. At least superficially, age discrimination law *seems* to point in two opposite directions. On the one hand, there are social forces clearly at work: the gray lobby, the civil rights movement. On the other hand, the living law of age discrimination seems much freer of background than one would expect. There is very little in its history to explain why the law came about. There was no obvious pulling and hauling. There is only a dim, feeble background; yet, since the laws were enacted, the field has been growing rapidly and shows a great deal of vigor and life. How did this happen? Was it the logic of the law, the analogy with sex or race, the language of the texts? Does age discrimination law merely piggyback on the other civil rights laws? Is it nothing but a conceptual extension? Some evidence points in this direction. The laws seem careless, almost accidental. They come out of (almost) nowhere; like Topsy, they "just growed."

Yet there is another way to look at these laws. Their "legislative history," to be sure, does not explain much. But this may be because age discrimination is, as it were, a stand-in for other, broader norms—norms not recognized, or not yet recognized, in the legal system (certainly not in federal law). The legal system is, I think, full of such rules. They have not gotten their just due. This is an excuse for adding one more term to legal jargon: stand-in rules.

## On Stand-in Rules

All legal rules, of course, rest on general social norms. The relationship can be direct or indirect; the chain can have one or many links. The Food and Drug Administration has a rule that only 15 percent of the cherries in frozen cherry pie may be "blemished with scab, hail injury, skin discoloration, scar tissue or other abnormality."[239] Of course no "general social norm" dictates this rule about cherries. But it is easy to trace the steps *from* general social norms—about public health and safety, consumer fraud, and so on—*to* the rule about cherries.

In this case, there were many steps between the starting point in society and the ending point as an actual rule. This means that along the way choices had to be made about how to translate norms and demands into workable tools. The frozen cherry rule is of a type people tend to call "technical" or "instrumental." The rule goes back to general principles, but it is not a principle itself. It does not produce analogies, it does not grow, it has no emotional or normative content of its own. Its normative strength is derivative.

Thousands of rules (and rules and regulations) in the legal system are "technical," like the rule about cherry pie. They are detailed, quantitative, specific. The speed limit is an everyday example. Not that detailed, quantitative rules are inherently "technical." Currently, the debate over the national speed limit of 55 miles per hour shows that a "technical" rule can come to stand for some larger principle and generate considerable heat. So, too, of retirement age, of course.

Thus some rules are purely "technical"; others change and develop because they express some general principle directly, some social norm. Still others—and this is the case before us— do not express social norms directly; but people see them or use them as stand-ins or substitutes for a social norm which the law, for one reason or another, does not recognize. These rules, in other words, owe their "success" to the social norm for which they "stand in," as substitute or symbol.

The process of legal change, over time, often appears ragged, illogical, full of pointless zigs and zags. Usually, it is not quite so chaotic as it seems. Social forces are at work, but they tug and pull in opposite directions. Obviously, there is no simple way for law and legal process to absorb and digest general social norms. (By general social norm all that is meant is a feeling or idea shared by most people in some social group.) Wants, demands, and interests work directly on law-making bodies. But vague feelings of right and wrong do not have lobbies. They turn into law in slower, less dramatic ways.

Let us assume that there is, today, a social norm along the following lines: if a product or a machine hurts an innocent person, that person ought to receive some sort of payment. People know that life is unfair; that accidents happen (even if they are nobody's fault); but when a person is so unlucky as to suffer some terrible injury at work or on the street, there should be recompense. Life should not be *doubly* unfair.

There is of course no such *legal* principle and never has been. There is no general principle of compensation for injury or redress for loss, no cradle-to-grave welfare. Why not? One can think of all sorts of reasons. One is that this "principle" would be expensive to put into operation, and hence business opposes it. People who hold the norm have not given much thought to how to put it into effect or who would pay for it. General social norms need not be rational and consistent with each other. Usually they are nothing of the sort. They are like political opinions: people are capable of espousing at the same time quite contradictory ideas—to cut taxes to the bone and increase public services, for example.

The hypothesis is this, then: when the law cannot completely absorb and express a general social norm—either because there is opposition, because of unarticulated inconsistencies, or because of problems of cost or administration—stand-in rules are likely to develop, in various corners of the system. The "norm" of full compensation is not and cannot be part of the law, but its influence shows all over tort law and in related fields.

Consider, for example, workmen's compensation. It started out as a program to deal with the problem of industrial accidents.[240] The root image or picture was the nineteenth-century factory: vast, dirty, noisy, and dangerous; full of blind and malevolent machines; and owned by distant, heartless capitalists. The workman earned his bread in the factory; when the machines mangled or crippled him, they destroyed his income as well as his body.

This was the background out of which compensation statutes grew; and the interest groups that struggled to frame a program were standard industrial actors—labor unions and organized management. But modern case-law and, to some extent, the laws themselves have wandered quite far afield: compensation for heart attacks; recovery for traveling salesmen who are injured in motel fires; doctrines about accidents on parking lots, at company picnics, and so on; not to mention recovery for losses (like disfigurement) that have nothing to do with making a living. Most of the statutes were passed during or just after World War I. By the 1930s and 1940s, the basic principles had become quite expansive. Courts talked about "liberal" construction. In one Idaho case, a crazed gunman burst into a Chinese restaurant, shooting; bullets injured a dishwasher. In a Wisconsin case, a truck driver, careless to say the least, urinated off the running board of a semi-trailer truck going thirty miles an hour; he fell and injured himself. In both cases, the company was liable for compensation.[241] This is indeed "liberal" construction. Yet there is a social and legal paradox: if I fall down the stairs at work (no fault of the company), I collect; if I fall down the stairs in my home, I get nothing.

There is no logical answer to the paradox. Workmen's compensation law, at the fringes, is stand-in law. It is a piece, a fragment, of a principle that does not exist, at least not as a principle of law. This is the rule of general compensation—that there should be recompense for any injury, so long as the victims are innocent themselves. There is no such legal rule, but there is a social norm, a common feeling of what is fair and right, an expectation. The feelings may never generate corresponding rules, for reasons of cost, perhaps, or problems of administration. But its normative power influences workmen's compensation, nudges it in one general direction. Workmen's compensation rules are half-a-loaf law (or slice-of-bread law), standing in for the larger principle.

Of course, workmen's compensation rules are not *officially* grounded on this fact. No one defends them as bits and pieces of a larger (but unrecognized) principle. They have their own justification, in terms of "policy." The cases talk about "liberal" interpretation, about "trends," about expanding coverage. This is natural and expected. In some fields, bits and pieces of stand-in law may get thicker and denser, and ultimately *become* the new principle. This is one way the common law grows. A classic technique of judges is to knit together these bits and pieces, then express the new pattern as a rule. This was a technique used in the famous essay by Warren and Brandeis, in 1890, on the right of privacy. They gathered up a rag and a bone and a hank of hair, from here and there in the case reports, and fashioned a brand new tort out of the fragments.[242]

Warren and Brandeis played the game in a way now out of

style: they announced a new principle, but hinted that in some sense it was already *there*, implicit or immanent in the common law. The modern "realist" could never accept this. In fact, Warren and Brandeis were describing a pattern or trend; the isolated cases they found were stand-ins, hinting at a broader principle which the law did not recognize, for whatever reason. The fragments never did come together, despite Warren and Brandeis, for many years, if they ever coalesced at all.

Much of modern tort and welfare law has developed through stand-ins. Tort law is a patchwork of doctrines. It approaches, but certainly does not reach, a general principle of recovery, for consumers, drivers, pedestrians, workers. There is nothing inevitable or irreversible about the trend. The "ultimate" principle may never grow into law. One can see it coming, at the end of a line on some imaginary graph; as a sort of limit of an infinite series, which approaches but never quite makes it. Here the analogy must stop. There is nothing mathematical about the legal system. The trend can, at any time, veer off to left or right—or go backward. The "ultimate" principle will come closer only if things go on as before, which they rarely do. The very concept of a "trend" can be misleading. The terms suggest something frictionless, moving through space. It focuses our eyes on the rolling ball, not on what the ball is rolling on, through, or over—on the forces pushing and pulling in various directions.

Age discrimination law is, I think, a double stand-in; it approximates *two* large (and unrecognized) principles. The first might be called the *civil rights* principle. This is the idea that people deserve to be judged for themselves alone, for inner or personal qualities, not for "immutable" characteristics like race, sex, or age, or for that matter, any other "unfair" criterion. The second is the *tenure* principle: people gradually develop (or should develop) vested rights, over time, to their jobs, homes, and other long-standing arrangements or relationships. Of course leases expire, jobs are held "at will," and so on; but the social norm treats these, in the proper case, as unfair technicalities.

The point is not that the principles are good or bad, or even that they make sense. In many ways, they are unexamined and inconsistent. It is child's play to poke holes in the civil rights principle, or the tenure principle. Also, landlords and employers resist. The norms are only half-conscious. People do not debate them, or think them through, or tote up the costs and dysfunctions. But the norms are social reality for many people, including judges and lawyers, vague and unformed as the norms are. They can be seen at work in the developing law.

Age discrimination rules thus develop along lines best explained as stand-ins for the super-rules or norms just mentioned. This is not "autonomous" legal growth. It is not best explained in logical, conceptual, analogical terms, from existing legal materials; it is not internal to the legal system; it is not "accidental" law, not the virgin birth it seems. Rather, it is stand-in law. The social force is diffuse, less palpable than the rage and passion underlying black civil rights. But that does not mean *no* social force lies behind it.

With stand-in rules, the underlying norm stays hidden, implicit. It hooks itself to another norm or a text—that is, to rules already strong and legitimate. Stand-in rules *look* like logical extensions—natural emanations from existing law. Only when there are many of these bits and pieces does the pattern become more obvious.

This may never happen, to be sure. Norms also have enemies. They benefit some people and injure others; they cost money; they pose problems; there are countervailing values. I make no prediction about the future. The point is simply this: the law of age discrimination, despite appearances, is not an accident. It is as exogenous as a rivers and harbors bill, or a major tax law. It is the product of outside force, though in a muffled and subtle way. Here as everywhere, society is the ultimate arbiter of law.

# Postscripts

*Postscript I  A No-Retirement Law in Action*

In Part II, it was noted that some states, including California, have abolished mandatory retirement. The California law is relatively new; it may be too soon to know the ultimate impact. But what has happened in the short run?

To find out, we surveyed a number of employers in northern California. The sample was not random; but we tried to get information from a range of firms and agencies. A questionnaire was sent to 31 personnel departments; when (as usual) answers dribbled in rather slowly, a follow-up letter was sent out. In the end, there were 21 responses, a response rate of 68 percent. The sample consists of 17 private employers and 4 public ones. Nine of the businesses and all of the public employers are located entirely in California. Eight businesses are interstate. (For two of these, the personnel director was able to give us information about his division only.)

In some ways, very little was learned from the responses. The law is either too new or too little known, or the companies simply do not intend to change their ways very much. Most companies, apparently, will keep the idea of a "normal" retirement age, usually the age at which employees once *had* to retire. The most popular "normal" age is 65. At least 15 companies used this age before the 1978 law. In a few cases, the "normal" age has changed since the law was passed.

We asked whether the employer made some attempt, formal or informal, to find out the retirement plans (or no-plans) of employees as they got close to "normal" retirement. Twelve did; 9 did not. There was some tendency for bigger companies (over 500 employees in California) to do so, compared with smaller companies.

We asked what steps a worker had to take to keep working after "normal" retirement age. In 9 businesses, the answer was simple: nothing. The worker merely kept on working. In 4 cases, the worker had to tell the supervisor that he planned to stay on. In 6 cases, the worker had to notify a personnel or employee benefits department. In 2 public agencies, the procedures were somewhat more elaborate.

The literature is full of discussions about how to handle employees who are "over the hill"; and the supposed cruelty of weeding these people out. We asked about this; no company mentioned it as a problem. Only one of the 21 has any routine, age-based tests; several others reserve the right to test particular employees who want to keep on working. Only 8 of the 21 have any procedure at all for dealing with "over the hill" workers. These 8 mention performance evaluations, physical examinations, and even in one case certifications of competence. Details are lacking, however, about the way these are carried out and how often they are used.

Respondents told us very little about a question that interested us greatly: that is, which people tend to stay on after retirement, and which do not? Seven respondents said that more men than women stayed on. None thought women were more likely to stay on, but the other respondents either did not know or saw no difference between the sexes. We also asked about married as opposed to unmarried workers. Only 4 respondents saw a difference; 3 of these thought married workers tended to stay on, 1 thought the unmarried did. Six saw a difference between low-paid and high-paid workers; 4 of these thought the low-paid tended to stay on; 2 thought the high-paid. (Not much can be made of numbers so small.) We asked about shop floor workers compared with office workers, or professional workers compared with clerical or sales. There were few responses; most said the groups behaved "about the same." The most popular response overall was "don't know." The new law has not had much impact on the work, or thinking, of personnel officers.

How many workers stay on past "normal" retirement? Six respondents said they did not know (this in itself is interesting). Nine said that most older workers did in fact retire at that point. Six employers said less than half actually gave up working. The respondents were in general quite vague; few gave any figures.

Respondents did not have strong feelings about the law. Most rather liked the idea. Some felt that workers retired anyway, and those that stayed on were useful and experienced. There were scattered opinions about costs or savings (in pension expenses); one respondent worried that younger workers might get frustrated, if their climb up the ladder was blocked. Some felt not enough time had gone by for sound evaluation, which is surely correct. In general, these people on the firing line do not feel that the sky is falling in—or, contrariwise, that something strange but wonderful has happened.

*Postscript II   The Big World*

One of the many problems with American scholarship—legal, social scientific, and historical—is its provincialism. Most of it seems to assume that the United States is a remote island, alone in the sea. Ignoring the rest of the world is more than bad taste; it can lead to dangerous error. A scholar might be struggling to explain some effects, using strictly American causes, when the same effects are occurring all over the world; conversely, he might adopt some global explanations (in terms of technology, or modern science), when the effect is quite peculiar to this country. One should at least ask, then, what the big world is doing about age discrimination.

It turns out that the United States *is* a bit of an island here, which strengthens the impression that American civil rights law, or some trait of American legal culture, is at least partly responsible. A survey, published in 1974, listed few laws outside the United States—Finland, Hungary, and Costa Rica were mentioned—that dealt with age discrimination in employment.[243] Finnish labor law forbids employers from discriminating on the basis of race, sex, age, or political and union activity.[244] Its impact is unknown to me. In the Federal Republic of Germany, a statute expresses the principle that workers should not be treated disadvantageously merely because they "exceed a given age-level."[245] Nothing in the standard commentaries suggests that this norm has much practical effect. Most countries do not seem to address "age discrimination" as a legal problem, in employment or otherwise. There are no such laws in Great Britain, France, or Italy, as far as I could tell. The few existing laws may or may not have some impact. Legal literature is mostly silent on this point.

One major exception is Canada. Age discrimination is prohibited by the Canadian Human Rights Act.[246] The provinces also tend to ban discrimination through Human Rights Codes, or the like. The Ontario Code prohibits discrimination on the basis of age, for those over 40 and under 65.[247] (The resemblance to ADEA is obvious.) The protected ages in Alberta are 45 to 65; in Prince Edward Island, 18 to 65.

The Manitoba Human Rights Act is especially broad. It outlaws age discrimination in jobs, housing, services, and advertising. The act has no age limitation, and the provincial Human Rights Commission takes complaints from all age groups. A relatively recent report (1981) mentions an employee who worked for a "large international drug company." At 65, he was retired against his will, in accordance with company policy. He turned to the Human Rights Commission. The company confessed it was "not aware of the provisions of the Human Rights Act in Manitoba." The complainant settled for a sizable lump sum payment ($65,000) plus adjustment of pension rights (he had meantime gotten another job).[248] Reports of other provincial commissions also make clear that, generally speaking, age discrimination law is by no means a dead letter. There are many complaints, and the trend, as in the United States, is up.

The Canadian situation is instructive in two rather contradictory ways. Canada, after all, had no equivalent of the American Bill of Rights, on a federal level, at the time these laws were passed. On the other hand, Canadian law unquestionably owes a good deal to American example. It developed in a framework of awareness of what was going on in American law.

Government reports and cases regularly cite American materials. The spirit of American law has radiated across the northern border, which culturally speaking is a flimsy barrier (no such influence flowed south into Mexico). The spread of American law took place even though some of the specific legal *structures* praised or blamed for American "legalization" had no exact counterpart in Canada.


*Postscript III    State Laws Against Age Discrimination*

Brief mention has been made, from time to time, of state laws against discrimination. Legal literature tends to neglect the state laws; it seems to assume that they are not terribly important. But this is almost surely wrong. A few states, of course, have no laws about age discrimination at all. Most states do, and their enforcement agencies almost certainly vary greatly in zeal and activity.

Some states put "age" on their list of forbidden criteria long before ADEA. Other states acted only after 1967, and presumably under the influence. It is generally the case (and why not?) that most energy and time are spent on race and sex discrimination. Nebraska, for example, established an Equal Opportunity Commission in 1965. In 1972, a new law banned "the practice of discriminating in employment against properly qualified persons because of their age."[249] For the fiscal year July 1, 1979–June 30, 1980, the commission recorded 656 "complaints" of employment discrimination. The largest category was "race or color" (262 complaints); next came sex (182); age was a poor third (83). But this is a growing category; it is already more important than "religion" (9 complaints) or "national origin."[250]

The picture in California is similar, though on a grander scale. In 1961, the state passed an act that made it unlawful to "refuse to hire . . . or to discharge, dismiss . . . or demote" any worker between 40 and 65 "solely on the grounds of age." At first, the Department of Human Resource Development was in charge.[251] California had adopted a Fair Employment Practices Act in 1959; in 1972 "age" was added to the list, and jurisdiction shifted to the Fair Employment Practices Commission. For 1976–77, the commission received over 13,000 complaints; 2,823 cases were "docketed and scheduled for formal investigation." Of these, 273 (9.6 percent) were age cases, lagging far behind race (1,200, or 42.5 percent) and sex (758, or 26.8 percent); again, age was much more significant than "creed" (2.3 percent). It was, however, not as important as "National Origin or Ancestry" (421, or 14.9 percent). This category is swollen with complaints from Hispanics, a large and sensitive group in California.[252]

There is a high degree of cooperation between EEOC and many of the state commissions; the Ohio Commission, which is a recognized "Deferral Agency" in a "deferral" state (see text, p. 21) has also had a "work sharing" arrangement with EEOC, under which cases filed with both agencies are divided between the two, "to avoid duplicated efforts."[253] In Connecticut, EEOC contracted in 1981–82 with the state commission to handle some 1,436 complaints, for which EEOC agreed to pay nearly $400 a head; and there was a similar arrangement in other states, for example, Minnesota.[254] Of course, most of these cases were race and sex cases, not age cases, but no doubt some age cases were included.

It is generally true that the number of age complaints is increasing. In Minnesota, there were 60 age complaints in the 1977–78 biennium to the Department of Human Rights (3 percent of the total); in 1979–80, there were 256 (13 percent); in 1981–82 there were about 381, and 227 of these were in fiscal 1982.[255] The category is far from trivial in the states that use it, for the most part. In a state like New York, complaints seem to be running currently at a rate of about 1,300 a year.[256] In North Carolina, however, the Human Relations Council received 22 complaints in 1982,[257] which is less than Idaho, a state with a much smaller population.[258]

The general rise in state activity parallels, of course, what is happening at the federal level, in both agencies and courts. Reported state cases are much fewer than federal cases; but the trend is definitely up. All this should come as no surprise. The states and the federal government are part of a single society. All parts share, on the whole, the same social and normative adventures; and the same social forces are at work.

# Acknowledgments

The project was generously, and patiently, supported by the Russell Sage Foundation; I want to express my appreciation to the Foundation and its officers for making the study possible. I also wish to thank the following for their help in the research: Joanne Abelson, Steven Arkin, Julia Baskett, Linda Cheng, Anne Doolin, Daniel Dorosin, Lauren Edelman, Dana Gross, Barbara Hurlburt, Bruce King, Peter Langerman, Guillermo Nodarse, Margaret Spencer, Susan Stefan, Leonard Swyer. I also appreciate the comments of Deborah Rhode, and the help of Professor Myron Jacobstein, Iris Wildman, and the staff at the Stanford Law Library; Mrs. Joy St. John gets special thanks for coping with endless drafts and redrafts of this study. Martin Levine, of the Law Center of the University of Southern California, made extensive and enormously helpful comments on the semifinal draft.

# Notes

[1] On the reality or nonreality of the litigation explosion, see Lawrence M. Friedman, "The Six Million Dollar Man: Litigation and Rights Consciousness in Modern America," *Maryland Law Review* 39 (1980): 661; Marc Galanter, "Reading the Landscape of Disputes: What We Know and Don't Know (And Think We Know) About Our Allegedly Contentious and Litigious Society," *UCLA Law Review* 31 (1983): 4; Jethro K. Lieberman, *The Litigious Society* (1981).

[2] David Clark, "Adjudication to Administration: A Statistical Analysis of Federal District Courts in the Twentieth Century," *University of Southern California Law Review* 55 (1981): 65.

[3] On prisoners' rights, there is a large literature. Typical of the older view is Ruffin v. Commonwealth, 62 Va. (21 Gratt.) 790, which referred to prisoners as "slaves" of the state, who had "forfeited" all "personal rights except those which the law in its humanity" granted them. Typical of the newer approach is the line taken in Procunier v. Martinez, 416 U.S. 396 (1974), that the courts will "protect" prisoners in cases where prison regulations or practices offend any "fundamental constitutional guarantee." For a case study of the development of "legalization" within a prison system, see James B. Jacobs, *Statesville: The Penitentiary in Mass Society* (1977).

[4] The literature on how the law affects old and middle-aged people is recent and rapidly growing. The subject is even insinuating itself into the law curriculum. See Martin L. Levine, "Legal Education and Curriculum Innovation: Law and Aging as a New Field of Law," *Minnesota Law Review* 65 (1981): 267. There is an extensive bibliography in the *Law Library Journal* 73 (1980): 271. Another bibliography is at *Hastings Law Review* 32 (1981): 1401. See also Martin L.

Levine, "Introduction: The Frame of Nature, Gerontology, and Law," *University of Southern California Law Review*, 56 (1982): 261; Leonard D. Cain, "Aging and the Law," in Robert H. Binstock and Ethel Shanas, eds., *Handbook of Aging and the Social Sciences* (1976), p. 342.

[5] The Age Discrimination in Employment Act is 29 U.S.C. 621; the Age Discrimination Act is 42 U.S.C. 6101.

[6] For an example, see N.Y. Exec. Law, sec. 296. There is a discussion of the state statutes in "Age Discrimination in Employment: the Problem of the Older Worker," *New York University Law Review* 41 (1966): 383.

The earliest statute was Colorado's, passed in 1903 (!). It stated that no business employing labor "shall discharge any individual between the ages of eighteen and sixty years, solely and only upon the basis of age," as long as the worker was "well versed in the line of business" carried on by the employer and was "qualified physically, mentally, and by training and experience, to satisfactorily perform and does satisfactorily perform the labor." Violators were liable to a fine. Laws Colo. 1903, p. 307. I have been unable to find any material that sheds light on the background of this act. Two age statutes were passed in the 1930s; all others date from the 1950s or later. There were twenty-three of these statutes in 1966, on the eve of the federal law. *New York University Law Review* op. cit., p. 388n.

[7] In 1975, there were 22,696,000 people over 65, constituting 10.5 percent of the population. In 1980, there were 25,714,000, or 11.3 percent of the population. *Statistical Abstract of the United States* (1984), p. 31. Every projection predicts still more growth.

[8] Generally, on the theory of social movements and legal change, see Joel F. Handler, *Social Movements and the Legal System: A Theory of Law Reform and Social Change* (1978); Mancur Olson, Jr., *The Logic of Collective Action* (1965); Terry M. Moe, *The Organization of Interests* (1980).

On old-age politics specifically see Carroll L. Estes, *The Aging Enterprise* (1979), ch. 4; see also W. Richard Scott, "Reform Movements and Organizations: The Case of Aging," in Sara B. Kiesler, James N. Morgan, and Valerie K. Oppenheimer, *Aging: Social Change* (1981), p. 331.

[9] See Jackson K. Putnam, *Old-Age Politics in California* (1970), ch. 4; Abraham Holtzman, *The Townsend Movement: A Political Study* (1963).

[10] Putnam, op. cit., p. 52.

[11] See Edwin E. Witte, *The Development of the Social Security Act* (1962), pp. 159–60. In the background was the great clamor over the Townsend plan; this put pressure on the administration to do something for the elderly. But Witte thinks that in many ways the influence of the Townsend plan was politically perverse. Congressmen were besieged with letters demanding adoption of something like the Townsend plan. But they could not vote for the plan, because they considered it harebrained. "As the situation developed, the congressmen could not get any credit through voting for old age assistance on the moderate basis provided for in the economic security bill, while they could not vote for the Townsend plan because they felt it would wreck the country."

[12] 49 Stats. 623, Social Security Act, sec. 202(d), August 14, 1935. Under the amendments of 1939, a retired worker was allowed to earn $15 a month before losing benefits, 53 Stats. 1367, Social Security Act Amendments, sec. 203(d)(i), August 10, 1939. See Wilbur J. Cohen, *Retirement Policies under Social Security* (1957). Cohen points out that unions and others were afraid that if pensioners did

not retire, their incomes would depress the labor market by "subsidizing wages" (p. 69).

[13] The phrase is from Bernice L. Neugarten and Joan W. Moore, "The Changing Age-Status System," in Bernice L. Neugarten, ed., *Middle Age and Aging* (1968), pp. 5, 18. Neugarten and Moore remark that this was a case where "a legal definition . . . itself had important influence upon the definition of a particular age-group. . . . In many . . . programs . . . [and] in the mass media, 65 has come to be the reference point by which to distinguish the old from the middle-aged." See also Cohen, op. cit., ch. 2 ("How Was 65 Selected as the Retirement Age?"). Perhaps the reference point will now shift to 70, in part because of ADEA.

[14] 1954 U.S. Code Cong. and Admin. News 3775.

[15] The bill proposed by the House would have reduced the exempt age to 65. This would have destroyed any incentive for pensioners to get out of the job market. The Senate refused to accept this rather radical change in the Social Security Act.

[16] Bruno Stein, *Social Security and Pensions in Transition* (1980), p. 18. If Social Security "is a form of saving, then it is difficult to explain" why people have to stop work "in order to receive their benefits." And because it does not cover income from dividends and so on, Social Security "favors the well-to-do" and thus "raises issues of equity."

[17] See Lawrence M. Friedman, "Social Welfare Legislation: An Introduction," *Stanford Law Review* 21 (1969): 217; Fleming v. Nestor, 363 U.S. 603 (1960). The psychological meaning of Social Security—the way workers look at it—may have changed recently, because of the tremendous debate over the financial problems of the program, which gives off the message: you may think your pension is absolutely vested, and totally safe; but you are wrong. Many younger workers today are apparently skeptical about whether they will ever live to collect Social Security.

[18] Anyone who doubts this is invited to read Muller v. Oregon, 208 U.S. 412 (1908), the landmark case which upheld an Oregon law limiting the hours "females" could work in factories or laundries. The majority opinion asserted that "woman has always been dependent on man." Her physical weakness and the requirements of motherhood "justify special legislation restricting or qualifying the conditions under which she should be permitted to toil."

[19] Shelley v. Kraemer, 334 U.S. 1 (1948).

[20] Brown v. Board of Education, 347 U.S. 483 (1954).

[21] N.Y. Exec. Law, sec. 296; Pa. Stats. Ann. tit. 43 secs. 951ff.

[22] New York State Commission against Discrimination, *Report of Progress, 1959* (1960). The commission also worked with employers to reduce the problem of age discrimination. The New Haven Railroad had maximum age provisions in fifty-two job categories. The commission went to work on the railroad, and as a result the railroad agreed to eliminate maximum age specifications for thirty-eight of these categories. The rest it felt were jobs that *needed* an age cap (physically demanding, operating jobs).

Further on state laws, see Postscript III, pp. 119–120. California adopted an age discrimination law in 1961, Laws Cal. 1961, ch. 1623.

[23] 79 Stat. 218 (act of July 14, 1965). The declaration of objectives mentioned "opportunity for employment with no discriminatory personnel practices because of age," but the act itself merely set up a modest program of grants to the states for planning, programs, and research.

[24] Robert Stevens and Rosemary Stevens, *Welfare Medicine in America: A Case Study of Medicaid* (1974), p. 24.

[25] Ibid., p. 47. Medicare and Medicaid were provisions of the "Health Insurance for the Aged Act," 79 Stat. 290 (July 20, 1965).

[26] In the current debates over Social Security, it seems clear that the program has, for the first time, lost some of its popularity; and this is because, I believe, there is a feeling now that the interests of the young and the old are adverse, or have become adverse—the young are paying too much; and many younger workers, it seems, doubt that Social Security will be around to take care of them when *they* reach 65.

[27] For example, "After forty-five it's hard to get a job," *U.S. News & World Report*, April 2, 1955, pp. 88–91; "Older worker: the U.S. must make better use of him," *Time*, October 19, 1953, p. 100.

[28] See, in general, Elizabeth Ann Kutza, *The Benefits of Old Age: Social Welfare Policy for the Elderly* (1981).

[29] Fay Lomax Cook, "Assessing Age as an Eligibility Criterion," in Bernice L. Neugarten, ed., *Age or Need? Public Policies for Older People* (1982), p. 171.

[30] 81 Stat. 602 (December 15, 1967); 29 U.S.C. 621.

[31] President Lyndon Johnson issued an executive order (No. 11141) on February 12, 1964, which declared it the "policy" of the Executive Branch that "contractors . . . engaged in the performance of Federal contracts shall not . . . discriminate against persons because of their age," or mention a "maximum age limit" in advertisements for workers, unless the age criterion is "based upon a *bona fide* occupational qualification, retirement plan, or statutory requirement." *Federal Register*, 29 (1964): 2477.

[32] The Senate originally fixed a minimum age of 45. The House, however, set it at 40; and the lower age was unanimously adopted in committee. Cong. Rec. 113 (1967): 31253. There was also some discussion of the "retirement" of stewardesses by airlines, which forced these women out of their jobs at 32 or 35. Eleven members of the committee filed a supplemental opinion to the report, expressing the view that such practices constituted age discrimination and should be covered by the bill. The majority felt that the stewardess problem was not important enough in itself to justify lowering the age of the protected class to 32. 1967 U.S. Code Cong. and Admin. News 2225.

[33] 92 Stat. 189 (April 6, 1978), amending 29 U.S.C. 631. The amendment continued to allow retirement at 65 of those who for at least two years had been in a "bona fide executive or a high policymaking position" and entitled to an annual retirement benefit of at least $27,000. Another exception was for employees who were 65 and were serving under a "contract of unlimited tenure . . . at an institution of higher education." 29 U.S.C. 631(e). This exception expired on July 1, 1982.

[34] Cong. Rec. 110 (1964): 13942, 2599. Representative Roosevelt spoke against adding age to the bill: "we are losing sight of the main purpose of the bill. . . . I am dedicated to trying to do something meaningful with respect to discrimination because of age. I would not ruin the bill to do so." Representative Rodino added that the bill was "hardly the proper vehicle to deal with this question." Ibid.

[35] Joseph T. Drake, *The Aged in American Society* (1958), p. 81.

[36] 78 Stat. 265 (act of July 2, 1964, sec. 715); Cong. Rec. 113 (1967): 31255.

[37] 1967 U.S. Code Cong. and Admin. News 2214; the report was called *The Older American Worker—Age Discrimination in Employment*.

[38] Cong. Rec. 113 (1967): 34743, 31512.

[39] This general thesis is not self-evidently true. It can be disputed; and indeed, Martin Levine, who made long and incisive comments on the next-to-the-last draft of this book, definitely disagrees. As a result of his comments, I watered down some of the statements in the text, but essentially stuck to my guns. There *was* a legislative history of ADEA, to be sure; but the question is how much weight to put on what actions by what actors, and how to interpret these actions. I leave it to the reader to judge the extent to which ADEA did or did not result from ordinary interest-group pressures.

[40] 89 Stat. 728 (act of November 28, 1975); 42 U.S.C. 6101. Peter H. Schuck, "The Graying of the Civil Rights Law: The Age Discrimination Act of 1975," *Yale Law Journal* 89 (1979): 27; Howard Eglit, "The Age Discrimination Act of 1975, as Amended: Genesis and Selected Problem Areas," *Chicago-Kent Law Review* 57 (1981): 915.

[41] Cong. Rec. 121 (1975): 9228, 9212. There was also talk about guaranteeing "that discrimination against the elderly . . . will not be tolerated," and that senior citizens would gain protection for their "fundamental rights." One congressman thought that the act might help "eliminate the false notion that becoming a senior citizen is synonymous with becoming useless and unwanted." Id., pp. 9212, 9230, 9227.

[42] See Lee E. Teitelbaum, "The Age Discrimination Act and Youth," *Chicago-Kent Law Review* 57 (1981): 969. Professor Teitelbaum refers to what he calls a "false analogy" between old and young people. The act, he says, "assumed that if old people are treated differently because of age and it is wrong to so treat them, it must also be wrong to treat young people differently from others because of age" (p. 1003); see also Martin L. Levine, "Comments on the Constitutional Law of Age Discrimination," *Chicago-Kent Law Review* 57 (1981): 108.

Some of the state statutes also apply to people of any age. One of these is New York (Exec. Law, sec. 296). At first, the State Commission on Human Rights ruled that the statute was applicable only to "discrimination based on *overage*." Note, *New York University Law Review*, op. cit. (n. 6), p. 389n. This policy no longer applies. In McLean Trucking Co. v. State Human Rights Appeal Board, 80 A.D.2d 809, 437 N.Y. Supp.2d 309 (1981), the State Division of Human Rights (and the court) upheld a claim by a 23-year-old, who was turned down for a job as a tractor-trailer driver because he was too young. (The minimum age was 24.)

[43] 92 Stat. 1555 (act of October 18, 1978); 42 U.S.C. 6101. Arguably, discrimination can mean simply making distinctions. If so, then it can be "reasonable" or "unreasonable." Martin Levine in a private communication stresses this point. Still, in civil rights laws, "discrimination" is exclusively understood, I think, as the bad sort; this is certainly what "race discrimination" means.

[44] ECOA is 15 U.S.C. 1691. See, for general treatment of the statute, Howard C. Eglit, *Age Discrimination* (1981), ch. 12. Some state statutes also cover credit, e.g., Ill. Rev. Stats. ch. 68, secs. 4-101 to 4-104. This law contains exceptions similar to those in the federal statute.

The elderly apparently played no role in the passage of ECOA, which was vigorously pushed by women's groups; see Joyce Gelb and Marian Lief Palley, "Women and Interest Group Politics: A Comparative Analysis of Federal Decision-Making," *Journal of Politics* 41 (1979): 362.

[45] Eglit, op. cit., ch. 11.

[46] The law is the Illinois Human Rights Act, Ill. Rev. Stats. ch. 68, secs. 1-102, 5-101.

[47] 88 Stat. 74 (act of April 8, 1974, sec. 28).

[48] The case was EEOC v. Wyoming, 460 U.S. 226, 103 S.Ct. 1054 (1983). A game warden in Wyoming, Bill Crump, was dismissed at the age of 55. The issue was whether the 1974 amendments were invalid, under the doctrine of National League of Cities v. Usery, 426 U.S. 833 (1976). Congress had extended the wage and hour provisions of national labor law to state employees; in *Usery* the Supreme Court held, somewhat surprisingly, that this could not be done; it encroached too much on the prerogatives of the states. In EEOC v. Wyoming, the (bare) majority distinguished the *Usery* case, though a bit feebly. To extend ADEA to state employees was a "valid exercise of Congress's powers under the Commerce Clause." The Court left undecided whether the amendment "could also be upheld as an exercise of Congress's powers under sec. 5 of the Fourteenth Amendment."

[49] 92 Stats. 189 (act of April 6, 1978); 29 U.S.C. 631(a). There was some discussion of the new age ceiling; but only two congressmen spoke out against it. It passed the House 391 to 6; the vote in the Senate was 62 to 10. Cong. Rec. 124 (1978): H2274, S4454. The discussion was mainly about mandatory retirement, which is understandable. One congressman argued that "existing law" was itself discriminatory: "only workers between 40 and 64 are protected from mandatory retirement," which (in his view) made the law "its own worst offender." Senator Domenici remarked that "the way the current law reads, we have actually institutionalized discrimination against workers over the age of 65." Cong. Rec. 123 (1977): 30,567; 34,321.

[50] Private lawsuits under ADA can be brought only after administrative remedies are exhausted, 42 U.S.C. 6104(e), 6104(f), though there are provisions for judicial review, 42 U.S.C. 6105. See Mittelstaedt v. Board of Trustees of the University of Arkansas, 487 F.Supp. 960, 965 (D.C.E.D. Ark., 1980), stating that ADA "creates no private cause of action." There are almost no reported cases. See text at n. 107.

[51] Under ADA, each federal agency is supposed to issue regulations and seek to "achieve compliance," 42 U.S.C. 6104.

[52] For the Plan, see 92 Stat. 3781 (1978); see also Carl E. B. McKenry, "Enforcement of Age Discrimination in Employment Legislation," *Hastings Law Journal* 32 (1981): 1157.

[53] "Age Discrimination in Employment: Available Federal Relief," *Columbia Journal of Law & Social Problems* 11 (1975): 281, 341.

[54] Interview with Eleanor Holmes Norton, conducted June 5, 1979, by Gerald L. Maguire, reported in *Seminar Briefs, National Conference on Age and Employment*, Chicago, June 25–26, 1979, p. 55. Norton went on to say that staff was very keen on the new development: "Yes, the staff has felt some frustration in the past because there have been innumerable occasions where one could see that a person who came in alleging one kind of discrimination might also have fallen victim to another kind." It helped such cases to have one central agency which could "put together all of the elements of a discrimination complaint."

[55] The language of the law, 29 U.S.C. 633(b), was far from clear, and some lower federal courts held that a person had a choice—state or federal; the act was read to mean only that if one chose to try the state first, there was a waiting period before one could sue in federal court. But the Supreme Court, in Oscar

Mayer & Co. v. Evans, 441 U.S. 750 (1979), held otherwise; the claimant must try the state agency first, if the state has its own version of ADEA or the like.

[56] During the waiting period (at least sixty days), when no action can be brought in federal court, ADEA permits concurrent state and federal administrative jurisdiction over the age discrimination claim. This is in contrast to the sequential procedure under Title VII; here "victims" must file with a state antidiscrimination agency before filing with EEOC. 42 U.S.C. sec. 200e-5(c). Under ADEA, grievants may file with state and federal agencies simultaneously or may file with the state before or after they file with EEOC. Oscar Mayer & Co. v. Evans, supra, n. 55. It is therefore possible for an employer and employee to be dealing simultaneously with federal and state administrative agencies—and also preparing for private litigation, which can begin when the sixty-day period ends. See James R. Northrup, *Old Age, Handicapped and Vietnam-Era Antidiscrimination Legislation* (1977), p. 38. In practice, there is probably a lot better coordination; EEOC works with state agencies and lets them have first crack at local cases.

[57] Usery v. Sun Oil Co. (Delaware), 423 F.Supp. 125 (N.D. Texas, 1976); Brennan v. Ace Hardware, 495 F.2d 368 (8th Cir. 1874).

[58] In Marshall v. Sun Oil Co., 605 F.2d 1331 (5th Cir. 1979), the court tried to define some of the necessary steps in conciliation: telling the employer what was expected of him and giving him a chance to make amends. In a number of cases, courts have quibbled over whether conciliation has to be "exhaustive" or merely "reasonable"; see, for example, Marshall v. Newburg R-2 School District, 469 F.Supp. 1030 (E.D. Mo., 1979). There are quite a few cases where courts have held that the agency has not met its duty to conciliate, for one reason or another. See, for example, Brennan v. Ace Hardware, 495 F.2d 368 (8th Cir. 1974).

[59] Marshall v. Baltimore & Ohio Railroad Co., 461 F.Supp. 362, 370 (D. Md., 1978); Marshall v. Sun Oil Co., 605 F.2d 1331 (5th Cir. 1979).

[60] Charles C. Edelman and Ilene C. Siegler, *Federal Age Discrimination in Employment Law* (1978), pp. 234–35.

[61] On the transformation of grievances into claims, see Richard E. Miller and Austin Sarat, "Grievances, Claims, and Disputes: Assessing the Adversary Culture," *Law & Society Review* 15 (1980–81): 525; William L. F. Felstiner, Richard L. Abel, and Austin Sarat, "The Emergence and Transformation of Disputes: Naming, Blaming, Claiming . . . ," *Law & Society Review* 15 (1980–81): 631.

[62] For the figures, see *17th Annual Report*, EEOC, FY1982 (April 1983), pp. 4–5. Between fiscal 1981 and 1982 age complaints had gone up from about 9,400 to 11,000.

It would be naive to argue that "discrimination in employment is . . . increasing" simply because the number of complaints is growing; yet such a point was made in James A. Antonucci, "Discrimination against the Elderly: A Prospectus of the Problem," *Suffolk University Law Review* 7 (1973): 917, 922. On "judicialization," see Lawrence M. Friedman, "The Six-Million Dollar Man: Litigation and Rights Consciousness in Modern America," *Maryland Law Review* 39 (1980): 661.

[63] Note the stress on "business." In EEOC v. City of Janesville, 630 F.2d (7th Cir. 1980), the police chief of Janesville, Wisconsin, decided to fight retirement. The retirement age (55) applied to *all* policemen, including him. The court pointed out that BFOQ applied to "businesses," not particular positions, like police

chief. Thus the chief did not make out a case by showing that youth was not a BFOQ for his job, so long as it was a BFOQ for policemen generally. A most dubious decision.

Contrast Aaron v. Davis, 414 F.Supp. 453 (1976), a district court case from Arkansas. Here an assistant fire chief and a district chief in Little Rock, Arkansas, won an age discrimination case against the city. An ordinance prescribed mandatory retirement for firemen at 62. The court admitted (as it had to) that firefighting is a dangerous job; but the two plaintiffs convinced the court that "they were able to handle the physical and psychological demands"; that older, more experienced firemen had a better safety record than young ones; and that "chronological and functional age are seldom the same." The court refused to apply BFOQ as a defense. The ordinance was just an example of "stereotyping"; it merely assumed that older firemen could not "cut the mustard." Plaintiffs were reinstated and given back pay.

In EEOC v. City of St. Paul, 671 F.2d 1162 (8th Cir. 1982), the Eighth Circuit rejected EEOC v. City of Janesville, in a case involving fire chiefs. A policeman lost his case on BFOQ grounds in Beck v. Borough of Manheim, 505 F.Supp. 923 (E.D. Pa., 1981).

On BFOQ in general see Deborah H. Combs, "Striking a Balance between the Interests of Public Safety and the Rights of Older Workers: The Age BFOQ Defense," *Washington and Lee Law Review* 39 (1982): 1371.

According to one authority, about two and a half million people work in "hazardous" jobs that call for "very early retirement." These jobs include air traffic controllers (here the problem is really stress), police, firemen, and pilots. Elizabeth L. Meier and Barbara B. Torrey, "Demographic Change and Retirement Age Policy," in Malcolm H. Morrison, ed., *Economics of Aging: The Future of Retirement* (1982), pp. 61, 77–82.

[64] 42 U.S.C. sec. 2000e-2(e).

[65] Massachusetts Board of Retirement v. Murgia, 427 U.S. 307 (1976).

[66] See Rosenfeld v. Southern Pacific Co., 444 F.2d 1219 (9th Cir. 1971). The plaintiff, Leah Rosenfeld, applied for a position of agent-telegrapher for the railroad, at Thermal, California. The company talked about long hours of work, the "heavy physical effort involved in climbing over and around boxcars to adjust their vents, collapse their bunkers and close and seal their doors," and a lot of heavy lifting. To no avail.

[67] Dothard v. Rawlinson, 433 U.S. 321 (1977). In part—if the Court can be taken at its word—the justices were worried about the *safety* of women guards: the prison was full of "sex offenders who have criminally assaulted women in the past," and there would also be a "real risk that other inmates, deprived of a normal heterosexual environment, would assault women guards because they were women."

In Gunther v. Iowa State Men's Reformatory, 612 F.2d 1079 (8th Cir. 1980), a federal court distinguished *Dothard* and let stand a district court decision that disallowed the BFOQ defense in another prison-guard case. The district court "found" that there was less of a security issue in Iowa than there had been in the *Dothard* case.

[68] New York State Division of Human Rights v. New York-Pennsylvania Professional Baseball League, 36 A.D.2d 364, 320 N.Y.S. 2d 788, 793–794 (1971).

[69] 442 F.2d 385 (1971).

[70] 14 C.F.R. sec. 121.383(c).

[71] Keating v. FAA, 619 F.2d 611 (9th Cir. 1979); Starr v. FAA, 589 F.2d 307 (1979). The rule and its background are discussed in some detail in Rombough v. FAA, 594 F.2d 893 (2d Cir. 1979). Murnane v. American Airlines, 667 F.2d 98 (D.C. Cir. 1981) upheld a maximum *hiring* age (30) for flight officers, in part on the strength of the bus company cases cited below. Older flight officers would not have time to reach captain's rank before the mandatory retirement age.

[72] This "clearest" case—the airline pilots—is actually controversial. The *pilots* do not take it lying down. Pilot organizations have constantly agitated for change; and in 1979, Congress passed a law (P.L. 96-171) to have the whole question studied again (93 Stat. 1285, act of December 29, 1979, ordering the Director of the National Institutes of Health, "in consultation with the Secretary of Transportation," to conduct the study). The Institute of Medicine of the National Academy of Sciences came out with a massive report in March 1981, *Airline Pilot Age, Health and Performance: Scientific and Medical Considerations.* The report is cautious and measured, but its basic thrust expresses skepticism about the need for a flat age limit. As of this writing, however, the pilots still have to go at 60.

[73] 499 F.2d 859 (7th Cir. 1974). In Brynton Cab Co. v. Dept. of Industry, 96 Wis.2d 396, 291 N.W.2d 850 (1980), the Wisconsin Supreme Court cited the bus company cases in turning down the complaint of a one-handed man who wanted a job with a cab company.

[74] 531 F.2d 224 (1976); see also Tuohy v. Ford Motor Co., 490 F.Supp. 258 (E.D. Mich., 1980). A state bus company case was Sposato v. Ambach, 453 N.Y. Supp.2d 149, 114 Misc.2d 942 (1982), upholding the forced retirement of school bus drivers at 65.

[75] 567 F.2d 1267 (4th Cir. 1977).

[76] Smallwood v. United Air Lines, 661 F.2d 303 (4th Cir. 1981); cert. den., 456 U.S. 1007 (1982).

[77] See Adams v. Leatherbury, 388 So.2d 510 (Ala., 1980). In Civil Service Board of Portland v. Bureau of Labor and Industries, 61 Ore. App. 70, 655 P.2d 1080 (Ore., 1982), a maximum hiring age (32) in Portland, Oregon, for "fire fighters" was upheld. The court said that wherever there is a "substantial public safety factor," the employer can use BFOQ, so long as it has a "reasonable basis" for thinking that the likelihood of injury or death would increase if it changed its rule. Fire fighting is "an exceptionally arduous and hazardous occupation"; it takes eight or nine years for a fire fighter "to reach optimum proficiency"; after 40, "the aging process produces a negative effect on his performance"; and "older members of the fire companies" experience more than their share of "serious, long-time injuries."

[78] 553 F.2d 561 (8th Cir. 1977); cert. den. 434 U.S. 966 (1977).

[79] See the text discussion of Vance v. Bradley, 440 U.S. 93 (1979), pp. 85–86.

[80] See Ill. Ann. Stat., ch. 95 1/2, secs. 6-103(9), 6-109 (applicants who are over 69 have to show "ability to exercise ordinary and reasonable control of . . . a motor vehicle"); Me. Rev. Stat. Ann. tit. 29 secs. 542, 545-A, 545-B (special eye tests for those over 65; full driving tests for those over 75, even for renewals); see also Md. Transp. Code Ann. sec. 16-103(1)(9); La. Rev. Stat. Ann. sec. 32:403.1.

[81] 347 U.S. 483 (1954). There is, of course, an enormous literature on this famous case. A good account of the background is in Richard Kluger, *Simple Justice* (1976).

[82] Plessy v. Ferguson, 167 U.S. 537 (1896), upheld a Louisana Jim Crow law

131

and launched the "separate but equal" doctrine; Berea College v. Kentucky, 211 U.S. 45 (1908), upheld a Kentucky law which *required* segregation of schools, thus forcing an unwanted segregation on Berea College.

[83] For example, art. 8, sec. 207, of the Mississippi Constitution provided that "separate schools shall be maintained for children of the white and colored races." Mississippi also provided for segregated trains, buses, and jails; and made it a misdemeanor to publish arguments "in favor of social equality or of intermarriage between whites and negroes." Miss. Code 1942, sec. 2339.

[84] Mayor of Baltimore v. Dawson, 350 U.S. 877 (1955), affirming, *per curiam*, Dawson v. Mayor of Baltimore, 220 F.2d 386 (4th Cir. 1955), and outlawing segregated public beaches and bathhouses; see also Holmes v. Atlanta, 350 U.S. 879 (1955), another *per curiam* decision (on public golf courses), vacating Holmes v. City of Atlanta, 223 F.2d 93 (5th Cir. 1955), which tried to maintain the old "separate but equal" arrangement.

[85] 401 U.S. 424 (1971).

[86] New York City Transit Authority v. Beazer, 440 U.S. 568 (1979). In part, there was a failure of proof in this case. For example, 35 percent of the methadone users were in private programs, but plaintiff's evidence about blacks and Hispanics was about public programs only.

[87] Geller v. Markham, 635 F.2d 1027 (2d Cir. 1980); cert. den., 451 U.S. 945 (1981); see also Franci v. Avco Corp., 538 F.Supp. 250 (D.C. Conn., 1982); Pamela S. Krop, "Age Discrimination and the Disparate Impact Doctrine," *Stanford Law Review* 34 (1982): 837.

[88] Krop, op. cit. (n. 87), p. 850.

[89] Edelman and Seigler, op. cit. (n. 61), pp. 192–95.

[90] Julia Lamber, "Theoretical Perspectives on the Use of Statistics in Employment Discrimination Cases," paper delivered at the 1981 annual meeting, Law and Society Association, Amherst, Massachusetts, June 12–14, 1981; Marcy M. Hallock, "The Numbers Game—the Use and Misuse of Statistics in Civil Rights Litigation," *Villanova Law Review* 23 (1977): 5; Gregory L. Harper, "Statistics as Evidence of Age Discrimination," *Hastings Law Review* 32 (1981): 1347.

[91] See Personnel Administrator of Massachusetts v. Feeney, 442 U.S. 256 (1979), which was an attack on the Massachusetts Veterans Preference law, on the grounds that it discriminated against women "in violation of the Equal Protection Clause of the Fourteenth Amendment." Title VII of the Civil Rights Act of 1964, the basic federal sex-discrimination law, was no use to the plaintiff, because it specifically exempted veterans' preference laws, 42 U.S.C. sec. 2000e-11.

The Supreme Court upheld the Massachusetts law, even though it operated "overwhelmingly to the advantage of males," partly because "nothing in the record" suggested that the veterans' preference law was "originally devised or subsequently re-enacted because it would accomplish the collateral goal of keeping women in a stereotypic and predefined place in the Massachusetts Civil Service."

[92] *The Age Discrimination Study, Part II*, a Report of the U.S. Commission on Civil Rights, January 1979.

[93] See, for example, Marshall v. Sun Oil Co., 605 F.2d 1331 (5th Cir. 1979).

[94] 554 F.2d 730 (5th Cir. 1977). Sometimes, of course, the policy really is discriminatory, and is pervasive. See EEOC v. Sandia Corporation, 639 F.2d 600

(10th Cir. 1980). The court called this case "unusual" because of the company's "impersonalism and inconsiderateness toward human dignity" (p. 624). There was a good deal of evidence besides the statistical case.

[95] Mistretta v. Sandia Corp., 15 F.E.P. Cases 1690, 1711 (D.C. N.Mex., 1977). This was also a "battle of the statisticians" case, with such heavy missiles as the Kolmogorov-Smirnov Test and "discriminant analysis" flying through the air.

[96] Walter B. Connolly, Jr., "The Legal Implications of Layoffs and Terminations," in *Age Discrimination* (1982), pp. 63, 100. See also Edward F. Mannino and Marguerite S. Walsh, "How to Defend Age Discrimination Claims Through Personnel Practices and Litigation Strategies," *Practical Lawyer*, September 1982, p. 35.

See Cova v. Coca-Cola Bottling Co. of St. Louis, 574 F.2d 958 (8th Cir. 1978). Cova (age 62) and others were fired from their jobs in a shake-up and replaced by younger workers. They lost in the lower court and argued on appeal that defendant did not meet its burden to produce "legitimate non-discriminatory reasons for the discharges," because its evidence was (oral) testimony, not based on "fair formal evaluation procedures." But the court refused to rule that "formal records" are "required as a matter of law" by ADEA. See Schulz v. Hickok Mfg. Co., 358 F.Supp. 1208 (E.D. Ga., 1973), where the lack of a "formal letter of discharge setting forth the reasons for . . . termination" helped tip the scale. See also Michael H. Schuster and Christopher S. Miller, "Performance Evaluations as Evidence in ADEA Cases," *Employee Relations Law Journal* 6 (1981): 561.

[97] McDonnell Douglas v. Green, 411 U.S. 792 (1973), dealing with Title VII of the Civil Rights Act of 1964.

[98] Sutton v. Atlantic Richfield Co., 646 F.2d 407 (9th Cir. 1981). In general, the federal courts hold that Title VII principles apply to ADEA, whose provisions are almost "identical" to those of the 1964 law. Hodgson v. First Federal Savings and Loan Association, 455 F.2d 818, 820 (5th Cir. 1972).

The guidelines, of course, have to be reworded for ADEA purposes. See Cova v. Coca-Cola Bottling Co. of St. Louis, 574 F.2d 958 (8th Cir. 1978); Harpring v. Continental Oil Co., 628 F.2d 406 (5th Cir. 1980); Mark I. Schickman, "The Strengths and Weaknesses of the McDonnell Douglas Formula in Jury Actions under the ADEA," *Hastings Law Journal* 32 (1981): 1239.

[99] See McCorstin v. United States Steel Corp., 621 F.2d 749 (5th Cir. 1980).

[100] Michael H. Schuster, "Analyzing Age Discrimination Act Cases," *Law and Policy Quarterly* 4 (1982): 339; 73 percent of the cases in Schuster's sample were brought by individuals; the rest were brought by the government. The number of reported cases was definitely on the increase. The first eight years of ADEA (1968–75) accounted for 28 percent of the cases; 72 percent came in 1976–78. Ibid., p. 346.

[101] Assuming this is so, we have to ask *why* women prefer to base their claims on sex discrimination rather than on age discrimination. The answer may lie in differences in procedures—or in differences in perception. Women may honestly feel they are discriminated against because they are women, rather than because they are over a certain age. And of course they may be right.

It is also worth noting that the imbalance is *much* greater in the litigated cases than it is in complaints to EEOC. In fiscal 1981, 5,797 men and 3,302 women filed complaints under ADEA. Stephen R. McConnell, "Age Discrimination in Employment," in Herbert S. Parnes, *Policy Issues in Work and Retirement* (1983), pp. 159, 167.

[102] Schuster, op. cit. (n. 100), p. 342.

[103] Simmons v. McGuffey Nursing Home, Inc., 619 F.2d 369 (5th Cir. 1980).

[104] The case is Goldman v. Sears, Roebuck and Co., 607 F.2d 1014 (1979); the district court dismissed on procedural grounds, and the circuit court affirmed.

In LaRue v. General Telephone Company, 545 F.2d 546 (5th Cir. 1977), LaRue, an engineer in the "land acquisition group," applied for a job as senior engineer, which had fallen vacant. He did not get the job, which went, instead, to a younger man. LaRue claimed age discrimination and sued. The court, in a curt, *per curiam* decision, affirmed a summary judgment against him: "a review of the entire record has revealed not a scintilla of evidence concerning discrimination." This was also, significantly no doubt, a *pro se* proceeding.

[105] "News of Music: Lucine Amara and the Met," *New York Times*, February 5, 1981, p. 17, col. 4.

[106] In Rogers v. Exxon Research and Engineering Company, 404 F.Supp. 324 (D.C. N.J., 1975), Dilworth Rogers, a chemist, was forced to take early retirement at 60. He had worked for Exxon since 1938. After he lost his job, Dr. Rogers suffered from "severe abdominal pain, vomiting and impotency," brought on (according to his doctors) by the psychological grief he suffered. Dr. Rogers apparently fell apart; he burst out with many symptoms, all the way from itching skin rash through depression to inability to drive a car. These were "work-related" and got much worse when he lost his job, although a few symptoms "ameliorated."

The main issue in the case was whether the Rogers family should collect damages for pain and suffering (Dr. Rogers had meanwhile died). The trial court said yes. ADEA created a new "statutory tort," which gives the court the right to frame "a wide range of legal and equitable remedies," including damages for pain and suffering.

The Circuit Court reversed, in Rogers v. Exxon Research and Engineering Company, 550 F.2d 834 (3rd Cir. 1977); cert. den., 434 U.S. 1022 (1978). Congress specifically provided for the measure of damages: lost earnings. The courts were not to go beyond this; and damages for pain and suffering or emotional distress "cannot properly be awarded in ADEA cases."

[107] In NAACP v. Wilmington Medical Center, 491 F.Supp. 290 (1980), violation of ADA was alleged. This was part of a long, complex battle over "Plan Omega," a proposal to move the Wilmington Medical Center out to the suburbs. It was claimed that the move would have a discriminatory impact on blacks, Hispanics, old people, and the handicapped. The suit failed.

[108] Mittelstaldt v. Board of Trustees of the University of Arkansas, 487 F.Supp. 960, 965 (D.C.E.D. Ark., 1980).

[109] David H. Marlin, "Enforcement of the Age Discrimination Act of 1975," *Chicago-Kent Law Review* 57 (1981): 1049.

[110] Surprisingly, some of these are quite old, for example, N.J. Stat. Ann. 2A:170-92, which goes back to 1898; a more recent addition is Mass. Gen. Laws Ann. ch. 151B, sec. 4.11; Ill. Rev. Stats. ch. 68, sec. 3-104 (children under the age of 14 years); an example of a city ordinance is San Francisco's Municipal Code, pt. 11, art. 1.2 (1975). On the question of the reality or unreality of the underlying problem, see James P. Zais, "The Housing of Families with Children: Basic Trends," in Richard R. Nelson and Felicity Skidmore, eds., *American Families and the Economy: The High Costs of Living* (1983), pp. 183–208.

[111] Marina Point, Ltd. v. Wolfson, 30 Cal. 3d 721, 640 P.2d 115 (1982). The United States Supreme Court denied certiorari.

[112] Moses v. Falstaff Brewing Company, 550 F.2d 1113 (8th Cir. 1977).

[113] N.J. Stats. Ann. 2A:18-61-1. This is only the most obvious example of what seems to be a new principle developing in the law of landlord and tenant: a principle which would "prevent landlords from terminating or refusing to renew leases unless they affirmatively can show good reasons for so doing." Mary Ann Glendon, "The Transformation of American Landlord-Tenant Law," *Boston College Law Review* 23 (1982): 503, 542–45; Edward H. Rabin, "The Revolution in Landlord-Tenant Law: Causes and Consequences," *Cornell Law Review* 69 (1984): 517.

The United States is actually quite a laggard in this regard; many countries offer far more security to tenants against eviction.

[114] See Brian Berger, "Defining Public Policy Torts in At-Will Dismissals," *Stanford Law Review* 34 (1981): 153; Note, "Protecting At Will Employees against Wrongful Discharge: The Duty to Terminate Only in Good Faith," *Harvard Law Review* 93 (1980): 1816. There is a comprehensive treatment in Donald H. J. Hermann and Yvonne S. Sor, "Property Rights in One's Job: The Case for Limiting Employment at Will," *Arizona Law Review* 24 (1982): 764. The matter has begun to worry employers, who wonder "how to protect themselves from lawsuits"; most of the complainants are "middle managers." *New York Times*, April 21, 1983, p. 29, col. 4; p. 34, col. 1; Hermann and Sor, op. cit., pp. 800–804.

[115] Fortune v. National Cash Register Co., 373 Mass. 96, 364 N.E.2d 1251 (1977).

[116] Cancellier v. Federated Department Stores, 672 F.2d 1312 (9th Cir. 1982). I am indebted to Linda Cheng for information about the facts underlying the case. The case was featured on the very popular television program "60 MINUTES," in November 1981. The trial was held in federal court in the Northern District, California, Case No. C 79 1591.

A fairness and "tenure" factor is important, I believe, in many age discrimination cases. Take, for example, Williams v. General Motors Corp., 656 F.2d 120 (5th Cir. 1981). This was an ADEA case, won at the trial court level, lost on appeal. The court, in a footnote, pointed out what it considered a serious confusion in plaintiffs' case—the notion that there was some connection between "seniority" and "age discrimination." In fact these two were "unrelated." This confusion "pervaded" the trial. For example, during closing argument, "plaintiffs' counsel further alluded to 'seniority,' stating: 'A lifetime of work at General Motors. . . . Is this the reward?' " (p. 130, n. 17).

[117] Peter H. Schuck, "The Graying of Civil Rights Law: The Age Discrimination Act of 1975," *Yale Law Journal* 89 (1979): 27; for a discussion of Schuck's thesis, see George J. Alexander, "Shucking Off the Rights of the Aged: Congressional Ambivalence and the Exceptions to the Age Discrimination Act of 1975," *Chicago-Kent Law Review* 57 (1981): 1009; Schuck responded in the same issue with "Age Discrimination Revisited," p. 1029.

[118] Patricia L. Kasschau, "Age and Race Discrimination Reported by Middle-Aged and Older Persons," *Social Forces* 55 (1977): 728. In an earlier study, "Perceived Age Discrimination in a Sample of Aerospace Employees," *Gerontologist* 16 (1976): 166, Kasschau also found widespread perceptions of age discrimination. In this study, she gathered data through a mail questionnaire sent to workers in one division of an aerospace firm who were over 45. (There was a rather poor response rate: about a third.) Thirty-six percent said yes to the general question: "Have you experienced discrimination on the basis of your age since

reaching middle-age?" Another 45 percent reported that they knew people who had been discriminated against because of age. On the other hand, Kasschau cites a paper by E. Kahana and others (1974), which came to the opposite conclusion, that is, that "older persons do not typically report a great deal of discrimination or personal rejection" (Kasschau, op. cit., p. 729).

It is of course no easy matter to try to measure "age discrimination" (as opposed to asking people whether they think there is such a thing). Erdman B. Palmore and Kenneth Manton, "Ageism Compared to Racism and Sexism," *Journal of Gerontology* 28 (1973): 363, tried to measure inequality in income and education between age groups (as well as between races and sexes). They found what they were looking for, that is, disparities in income between age groups. In fact, age group inequalities got worse between 1950 and 1970, but at least some of this (they felt) should be ascribed to "cohort differences between the aged and nonaged." (For example, old people were once young people, but they were young people at a time when fewer people in general finished high school or went to college.)

Teen-agers apparently feel that they are victims of age discrimination, according to at least one study. Almost *half* of all young people between 16 and 22 felt age discrimination had caused them trouble in getting a good job. Blacks reported this as a problem that faced them *twice* as often as race discrimination! David Shapiro, "Perceptions of Discrimination and Other Barriers to Employment," in Michael E. Boras, ed., *Pathways to the Future* (1981).

Public opinion surveys in 1974 and 1981 found that the overwhelming majority of Americans think that employers discriminate against older people. A survey of employers in 1981 confirmed this: 61 percent of the respondents believed that older workers were discriminated against. Stephen R. McConnell, "Age Discrimination in Employment," in Herbert S. Parnes, ed., *Policy Issues in Work and Retirement* (1983), pp. 159, 160–61.

[119]"Age Discrimination in Federally-Assisted Programs," Hearing before the U.S. Commission on Civil Rights, Washington, D.C., September 26–28, 1977, vol. 1, p. 12.

[120] Ibid., p. 14.

[121] James R. Northrup, *Old Age, Handicapped and Vietnam-Era Antidiscrimination Legislation* (1977), pp. 61–64.

[122] Eugene Bardach and Robert Kagan, *Going by the Book: The Problem of Regulatory Unreasonableness* (1982).

[123] *U.S. News & World Report*, September 12, 1980, p. 59.

[124] A cursory glance through help-wanted ads in newspapers before ADEA shows how pervasive the practice was. Here are a few out of countless examples: from the *New York Times*, January 22, 1950: "Clerks . . . Girls—Women . . . 28–35"; "Men . . . age 25 to 40 . . . temporary work with radio equipment"; "Advertising salesmen . . . not over 30 years." From June 21, 1956: "Sec'y to executive . . . to age 35 . . ."; "Clerical . . . 17–35 years . . ."; "Men! 21–50. . . ."

Needless to say, such advertisements have now completely disappeared.

[125] 29 C.F.R. sec. 860.92. The regulations also prohibit such specifications as "age 40 to 50," and the like. It is also dangerous under the regulations to advertise for "retired persons" or to say: "supplement your pension." Such language if "intended and applied so as to discriminate against others within the protected group" is unlawful. In other words, to ask for "retired persons"—who are usually in their 60s or over—discriminates against people in their 40s and 50s. See Barry B. Kaufman, "Preferential Hiring Policies for Older Workers Under

the Age Discrimination in Employment Act," *Southern California Law Review* 56 (1983): 825.

Under the Pennsylvania Human Relations Act, sec. 5(g), a person *looking* for a job was not allowed to place an ad specifying his "race, color, religious creed, ancestry, age, sex, or national origin." The Pennsylvania Supreme Court, in Commonwealth of Pennsylvania v. Pittsburgh Press Co., 483 Pa. 314, 396 A.2d 1187 (1979), declared this part of the law unconstitutional, under the First Amendment. The defendant in the case was a newspaper, which "abetted" the offense committed by the advertisers, when it ran "situations wanted" ads that said things like "white woman," "recent college grad, good looking, twenty-five years old," and "COLLEGE GRAD—Born again Christian with Bachelor's Degree."

[126] Brennan v. Aragon Employment Agency, Inc., 356 F.Supp. 286 S.D. N.Y., 1973), aff'd 489 F.2d 752 (2nd Cir. 1974); see Charles D. Edelman and Ilene C. Siegler, *Federal Age Discrimination in Employment Law* (1978), pp. 91–97.

[127] Hodgson v. Approved Personnel Service, 529 F.2d 760 (4th Cir. 1975). In Marshall v. Goodyear Tire and Rubber Company, 554 F.2d 730 (5th Cir. 1977), a 57-year-old salesman in a Goodyear retail store was fired, presumably because he was doing a poor job. The manager then placed an ad in a local newspaper asking young people between 19 and 26 to apply for the job. This of course was bad, and no doubt helped Reed, the salesman, win his case and get back pay from Goodyear.

[128] "Perhaps . . . an ad directed to 'laid-off automobile workers' would not infringe, even though most of those laid off may be younger because of seniority rules. But generally an appeal to a younger class is suspect" (Hodgson v. Approved Personnel Service, n. 127, p. 766).

[129] Some people are born with a handicap; most of us are not. However, we can also develop handicaps later on in life. How this fact affects the growth of special rights for the handicapped is an interesting question.

[130] Irving Rosow, *Socialization to Old Age* (1974), pp. 7–12; Joseph T. Drake, *The Aged in American Society* (1958), pp. 378–90; see also Richard B. Calhoun, *In Search of the New Old: Redefining Old Age in America, 1945–1976* (1978).

[131] Here I may add, for what it is worth, my own impressions, based on discussions with students in Stanford Law School, generally fairly liberal. With regard to age—but *never* sex and race—these students sometimes reject the "victim's" perspective. Some students dismiss the idea of abolishing mandatory retirement as sentimental, uneconomic twaddle. They are not generally sensitive to ageism, though they are sensitive to race and sex stereotypes. Old age may be part of their future, but they spend as much time worrying about it as the average smoker spends worrying about lung cancer.

[132] Bernice L. Neugarten and Gunhild O. Hagestad, "Age and the Life Course," in Robert H. Binstock and Ethel Shanas, eds., *Handbook of Aging and the Social Sciences* (1976), pp. 35, 52.

In August 1983, thirty-four Jewish doctors living in New York, refugees from the Soviet Union, filed a "formal complaint" with EEOC complaining of discrimination on the basis of age, national origin, and religion, against various hospitals and medical associations. The spokesman, Arkady Fishman, was 45; he had passed many tests and written 800 letters seeking a residency. He was turned down over 800 times. *New York Times*, August 27, 1983, p. 7, col. 5.

[133] The example is not frivolous. For five embarrassing minutes I once watched

on TV a beauty contest for grandmothers. These women, many of whom were beautiful in all sorts of ways, looked grotesque mincing about in bathing suits and dyed hair, just as a child looks grotesque dressed up like a grown-up. If this shows remnants of "ageism" on my part, so be it.

[134] See, for example, William R. Stanton, *The Leopard's Spots: Scientific Attitudes towards Race in America, 1815–1859* (1960); Stephen Jay Gould, *The Mismeasurement of Man* (1981).

[135] J. G. Wood, *Illustrated Natural History* (1883), pp. 18–20. The "Mongolian race," too, was "inferior in moral and intellectual qualities" and had "made but little progress in civilization or literary pursuits."

[136] Neal E. Cutler, "Political Characteristics of Elderly Cohorts in the Twenty-First Century," in Sarah B. Kiesler et al., eds., *Aging: Social Change* (1981), pp. 127, 150–51.

[137] James A. Craft, Samuel I. Doctors, Yitzchak M. Shkop, Thomas J. Benecki, "Simulated Management Perceptions, Hiring Decisions and Age," *Aging and Work* 2 (1979): 95, 101.

[138] In theory, a young person could complain about *benefits* to the elderly—on equal protection grounds, for example. In Thomas v. Pate, 493 F.2d 151 (7th Cir. 1974), black prisoners in a state penitentiary complained about a whole host of practices which they claimed were discriminatory. Race was the issue; but plaintiffs did throw in a complaint that "inmates at the prison who are under forty are not given free long underwear"; older prisoners (and, at other prisons, everybody) got this privilege free. This complaint got nowhere; the court refused to hold the practice "arbitrary"; it might be that the prison had some "rational basis" for this distinction between age groups (p. 162).

Suppose that an employer decided to give *preferences* to workers over 60. Could a 45-year-old complain, under ADEA? Is "reverse discrimination" legal or illegal under the act? This issue has not been resolved by the courts; for a discussion, see Barry B. Kaufman, "Preferential Hiring Policies for Older Workers under the Age Discrimination in Employment Act," *Southern California Law Review* 56 (1983): 825. The regulations seem to favor the notion that reverse discrimination is illegal; see 29 C.F.R. sec. 860.92 (n. 125).

[139] Howard Eglit and Bernice Neugarten, "Introduction" (to the symposium issue on age discrimination), *Chicago-Kent Law Review* 57 (1981): 805, 806.

[140] On the age of consent in California, for example, see Lawrence M. Friedman and Robert V. Percival, *The Roots of Justice: Crime and Punishment in Alameda County, California, 1870–1910* (1981), p. 139.

[141] I am indebted to Dana Gross for tracking down these laws. Representative cites: Ala. Code, ch. 1, sec. 2 (1823); Ga. Laws Dig. 429 (1837); Ill. Rev. Code 251 (1827); Me. Laws 1821, ch. 84, sec. 1.

[142] N.J. Stats. Ann. 2A:69-1 (1976).

[143] David H. Fischer, *Growing Old in America* (1978), p. 80. On retirement in general, there is an enormous (and growing) literature. Representative titles include James W. Walker and Harriet L. Lazer, *The End of Mandatory Retirement: Implications for Management* (1978); also, *Mandatory Retirement: The Social and Human Cost of Enforced Idleness*, Report, Select Committee on Aging, 95th Cong., 1st sess. (August 1977); William Graebner, *A History of Retirement: The Meaning and Function of an American Institution, 1885–1978* (1980); W. Andrew Achenbaum, *Old Age in the New Land* (1978); Robert C. Atchley, *The Sociology of Retirement* (1976); Cordelia Katherine W. Reimers,

"The Timing of Retirement of American Men" (Ph.D. thesis, Columbia University, 1977); Malcolm H. Morrison, ed., *Economics of Aging: The Future of Retirement* (1982); Carole Haber, *Beyond Sixty-Five: The Dilemma of Old Age in America's Past* (1983). For England, see Jill Quadagno, *Aging in Early Industrial Society: Work, Family and Social Policy in Nineteenth-Century England* (1982).

[144] For Kent's comments on this "very singular limitation," that is, the retirement provision, and quoting from Hamilton in *Federalist* 79, see 7 Johns. Ch. 346 (1823).

[145] Fischer, op. cit. (n. 143), p. 143.

[146] On the Procter and Gamble plan, see I. W. Howerth, "Profit-Sharing at Ivorydale," *American Journal of Sociology* 2 (July 1896): 43, 49–50.

[147] On the Baltimore and Ohio plan, and the history of pensions in general, see Haber, op. cit. (n. 143), pp. 113ff.; the Procter and Gamble plan is set out in an appendix to Paul U. Kellogg, *The Pittsburgh Survey* (1911), vol. 6, *Wage Earnings, Pittsburgh*, pp. 485ff.

[148] *Report of the Pennsylvania Commission on Old Age Pensions* (1919), p. 118.

[149] Latimer, *Industrial Pension Systems* (vol. 1, 1932), p. 74.

[150] *Industrial Pensions in the United States* (1925), p. 70.

[151] Robert M. Macdonald, *Collective Bargaining in the Automobile Industry* (1963), pp. 34–35. Ford's agreement resulted in the "establishment of the industry's first pension plan for hourly rated workers." The plan was noncontributory; it guaranteed a pension of $100 a month to employees who were 65 and had thirty years' service.

[152] Inland Steel Co. v. National Labor Relations Board, 170 F.2d 247 (7th Cir. 1948); cert. den., 336 U.S. 960 (1949).

[153] 88 Stat. 829 (act of September 2, 1974); see sec. 203(a), id., at 854.

[154] Under ERISA, then, the "right" to a pension from the private employer can vest in such a way as to become as firm as the right to insurance proceeds, that is, rights "vested" under a private contract. In legal theory Social Security pensions are not vested at all (see Flemming v. Nestor, 363 U.S. 603, 1960); psychologically and politically, however, this program has been—at least until now—as vested as vested can be. In general, the line between social insurance programs and private ones (these latter programs are encouraged and controlled by law, to be sure) blurs considerably.

[155] See Stanley Parker, *Work and Retirement* (1982), pp. 150–51, citing studies that suggest that most people are against forced retirement both for themselves and for others.

[156] E. Brewer, in *North American Review*, 166 (January 1898): 124. The article commended a retirement bill that had been introduced by Representative Brosius of Pennsylvania. Under this bill, a government worker could retire at age 60, after thirty years' service; the worker *had* to retire at 70, after thirty-five years' service.

[157] W. L. Stoddard, "More Federal Pensions," *New Republic*, March 6, 1915, pp. 125, 127.

[158] 41 Stats. 614, 617 (act of May 22, 1920).

[159] Ibid., at 617.

[160] William Graebner, *A History of Retirement: The Meaning and Function of an American Institution, 1885–1978* (1980), pp. 57, 62–63, 66–67, 74, 79.

[161] See, for example, Levy Anderson, "Vested Rights in Public Retirement

Benefits in Pennsylvania," *Temple Law Review* 34 (1961): 244, on the rise of retirement programs in that state.

[162] Robert M. Fogelson, "The Morass: An Essay on the Public Employee Pension Problem," in David Rothman and Stanton Wheeler, eds., *Social History and Social Policy* (1981), pp. 145, 151; Abraham Epstein, *The Challenge of the Aged* (1928), pp. 166–177.

[163] See Laws Mass. 1911, ch. 532; Laws Ill. (spec. sess.) 1915, p. 32, set up a commission to consider the whole pension issue; Laws Ill. 1921, pp. 203, 262, 388, established various municipal pension plans; see also Laws Me. 1919, ch. 38.

[164] See, for example, Robert Sherwood, *Roosevelt and Hopkins: An Intimate History* (1948), p. 69.

[165] 295 U.S. 330 (1935).

[166] Ibid., at 362.

[167] Ibid., at 364.

[168] Ibid., at 379, 381. Again, at 391: "it seems to be assumed that Congress could compel the dismissal of aged employees."

[169] Ibid., at 384. Brandeis, Stone, and Cardozo joined in the dissent.

[170] Lamon v. Georgia Southern and Florida Railway Co., 212 Ga. 63, 90 S.E.2d 658 (1955). Lamon also argued that he had been deprived of a property right without due process of law. But the court disagreed. Seniority is merely a creature of contract; it is not a vested right. The collective bargaining agreement, by its very terms, was subject to revision; so, in effect, plaintiff had already agreed in advance to the revision that forced him to retire from his job at the age of 70.

[171] 125 F.Supp. 441 (D.C.E.D. Tenn., 1954), aff'd 229 F.2d 578 (1956); cert. den., 351 U.S. 953 (1956).

[172] The court cited and quoted from an unpublished opinion of District Judge William J. Campbell, 1951, No. 51C 902, D.C.N.D. Ill., E. Div., Boget v. Chicago and Northwestern Railroad Co., which reached the same conclusion. For a similar result, see McMullans v. Kansas, Oklahoma & Gulf Railway Co., 229 F.2d 50 (10th Cir. 1956), aff'ing 129 F.Supp. 157 (D.C.E.D. Okla., 1955); United States Steel Corp. v. Nichols, 229 F.2d 396 (6th Cir. 1956).

[173] Evan K. Rowe and Thomas H. Paine, "Pension Plans under Collective Bargaining Agreements: II—Compulsory Retirement," *Monthly Labor Review* 76 (1953): 484. The authors surveyed 300 pension plans; 175 of them called for compulsory retirement, usually (60 percent) at age 65.

[174] Melvin K. Bers, *Union Policy and the Older Worker* (1975), pp. 69ff. Bers quotes a letter written by Walter Reuther in July 1952, which asserted UAW policy *against* mandatory retirement. Where pension plans had such features, Reuther claimed, it was "only because of management insistence"; the union "fought hard and long against compulsory retirement." But Bers claims that other unions were "indifferent" and that in 1953 some locals of oil refinery unions in the Bay Area actually "sponsored" compulsory retirement.

The United Mine Workers opposed compulsory retirement, and their national agreements prohibited it. Ewan Clague, B. Palli, and L. Kramer, *The Aging Worker and the Union: Employment and Retirement of Middle-Aged and Older Workers* (1971), p. 86.

[175] See, on New Deal labor legislation, Peter J. Irons, *The New Deal Lawyers* (1982), chs. 10ff.; Harry A. Millis and Emily Clark Brown, *From the Wagner Act to Taft-Hartley: A Study of National Labor Policy and Labor Relations* (1950).

[176] Herbert S. Parnes and Gilbert Nestel, "The Retirement Experience," in Herbert S. Parnes, ed., *Work and Retirement: A Longitudinal Study of Men* (1981), p. 155.

[177] According to one study, done around 1970, about a quarter of all working men were subject to mandatory retirement; and 30 percent of these men retired unwillingly. This means about 7 percent or so of the total male work force. The Department of Labor estimated that between 80,000 and 130,000 extra men would have been in the labor force, in 1976, except for mandatory retirement. Philip L. Rones, "Older Men—the Choice between Work and Retirement," *Monthly Labor Review* 101 (1978): 3. See also James H. Schulz, "The Economics of Mandatory Retirement," *Industrial Gerontology* 1 (Winter 1974): 1.

There seems to be no agreement whatsoever on the number of workers who want to stay on the job. A Sears, Roebuck study claimed that 45 percent of its employees would choose to work past 65 (*New York Times*, April 16, 1978). A Harris poll in 1979 found that 51 percent of employees surveyed wanted to work past the retirement age; a poll in 1982 showed that 64 percent of the people who were 65 and older planned to retire either after 70 or never—compared with 57 percent in 1974 (*New York Times*, March 4, 1979; February 13, 1982).

In any event, what does it really mean to say that a particular worker retired "voluntarily"? A book published in 1967 argued that about 80 percent of all retirements were "involuntary." This figure was arrived at by counting workers over 65 who did not work *and* had incomes below the poverty line. For retirement to be truly "voluntary," it must mean that "retirement is preferred to the alternative of participation in the labor force and that retirement carries with it at least a socially acceptable minimal income." Michael J. Brennan, Philip Taft, and Mark B. Schupack, *The Economics of Aging* (1967), pp. 222–24.

[178] Robert Clark, Juanita Kreps, and Joseph Spengler, "Economics of Aging: A Survey," *Journal of Economic Literature* 16 (1978): 919, 934–35.

See Dorothy R. Kittner, "Forced Retirement: How Common Is It?" *Monthly Labor Review* 100 (December 1977): 60. According to Kittner, in 1974 over 10 million workers were subject to mandatory retirement—about 45 percent of the workers that had "defined benefit plans." Kittner distinguishes between "compulsory retirement" (the employer can force the worker out, but can also keep workers on, on a year-to-year basis); and "automatic retirement," which means that the employer *cannot* "retain an elderly worker." Compulsory retirement was much more common. Kittner also reports that mandatory retirement was a feature of only 40 percent of the plans negotiated by unions, but 60 percent of the plans that were not negotiated by unions. See also Victor R. Fuchs, *How We Live: An Economic Perspective on Americans from Birth to Death* (1983), pp. 192–94.

[179] Harold L. Sheppard, "Work and Retirement," in Robert H. Binstock and Ethel Shanas, eds., *Handbook of Aging and the Social Sciences* (1976), pp. 286, 305; G. Hamilton Crook and Martin Heinstein, *The Older Worker in Industry: A Study of Attitudes Toward Aging and Retirement* (1958), ch. 6, pp. 48–56. The authors of this study (of California industrial workers) were surprised that so many workers, even older ones, accepted the idea of compulsory retirement; yet over half did not, or accepted it subject to qualification.

A Canadian study (593 employees in a service industry in Saint John, New Brunswick) reported (1979) that the overwhelming majority of workers (86.5 percent) wanted to retire at 65 or earlier; 4.4 percent did not respond. Only 9.1 percent wanted to continue working. Those with salaries over $30,000 showed less enthusiasm for retiring (68.4 percent); but other than this one group, salary level did not seem to make much difference. Unskilled laborers *all* wanted to retire; 94.7 percent of the skilled laborers; 86.3 percent of the clerical workers; 76.8 percent of the professionals. Beth Gilbert, Deborah Armstrong, and Judy MacLeod, "Mandatory Retirement in the Saint John Area: An Exploratory Study," unpublished report, New Brunswick Human Rights Commission, 1979, pp. 15–24. See also Parnes and Nestel, op. cit. (n. 176), pp. 164–65.

[180] Helen Baker, *Retirement Procedures under Compulsory and Flexible Retirement Policies* (1952), p. 22.

[181] Ibid., pp. 18, 21; see also Graebner, op. cit. (n. 160), p. 227.

[182] United Air Lines v. McMann, 434 U.S. 192 (1977). The Chief Justice wrote the majority opinion; Stewart and White wrote separate concurrences. Thurgood Marshall dissented, joined by Justice Brennan.

[183] Ibid., at 203. In the "context" of the statute, "subterfuge" had to have "its ordinary meaning and we must assume Congress intended it in that sense."

[184] Marshall, J., dissenting at 434 U.S 217.

[185] The amendment was in 92 Stats. 189 (act of April 8, 1978).

[186] The cases are McIlvaine v. Pennsylvania, 6 Pa. Comwth. 505, 296 A.2d 630 (1972); aff'd 454 Pa. 129, 309 A.2d 802 (1973); cert. den., 415 U.S. 986 (1974); Lewis v. Tucson School District No. 1, 23 Ariz. App. 154, 531 P.2d 199; cert. den., 423 U.S. 864 (1975); Armstrong v. Howell, 371 F.Supp. 48 (D.C. Neb., 1974); Aronstam v. Cashman, 132 Vt. 538, 325 A.2d 361 (1974).

[187] The plaintiff in the McIlvaine case, cited above, relied chiefly on the Pennsylvania Constitution (art. 1, sec. 26), and on the Pennsylvania Human Relations Act, 43 Pa. Stats. secs. 951ff., though he also cited the Fourteenth Amendment and ADEA. See also Fabio v. City of St. Paul, 267 Minn. 273, 126 N.W.2d 259 (1964).

[188] Belcher v. Gish, 555 S.W.2d 264 (Ky., 1977). The court dismissed the constitutional arguments; a teacher has no "vested right to employment to teach in the absence of contract."

[189] Nelson v. Miwa, 56 Haw. 601, 546 P.2d 1003 (1976). The Hawaii Board of Regents set 65 as a retirement age; exceptional people could be reappointed on a year-by-year basis, up to age 70. In Board of Regents of the University of Nevada v. Oakley, 637 P.2d 1199 (Nev., 1981), the court knocked out a mandatory retirement policy of the university on the grounds that it conflicted with a general statute on state personnel policy, which barred discharging "because of age"; see also Dolan v. School District No. 10, Deer Lodge County, 636 P.2d 825 (Mont., 1981).

[190] Nelson v. Miwa (n. 189), at 546 P.2d 1013.

[191] Comment, "Mandatory Retirement: The Law, the Courts, and the Broader Social Context," *Willamette Law Journal* 11 (1975): 389.

[192] Massachusetts Board of Retirement v. Murgia, 427 U.S. 307 (1976). Murgia, incidentally, was a lieutenant colonel in the Massachusetts police force and was hardly pounding a beat or rushing about in pursuit of criminals. Why such a person should be forced out at 50, law or no law, is hard to fathom.

[193] The doctrine that racial classifications are suspect and must be given "strict scrutiny" was first enunciated (ironically enough) in Korematsu v. United States, 323 U.S. 214 (1944), where the Supreme Court failed its own test and upheld the disgraceful removal of the West Coast Japanese during World War II. See Peter

Irons, *Justice at War: The Story of the Japanese American Internment Cases* (1983).

Sex discrimination cases are given some sort of in-between ("intermediate") scrutiny, Craig v. Boren, 429 U.S. 190 (1976), though it is fair to say that nobody is sure exactly what this means.

[194] Massachusetts Board of Retirement v. Murgia, 427 U.S. at 318 (1976). On the type of scrutiny exhibited in this case, see Martin L. Levine, "Comments on the Constitutional Law of Age Discrimination," *Chicago-Kent Law Review* 57 (1981): 1081, 1101–04.

[195] Vance v. Bradley, 440 U.S. 93 (1979).

[196] There is, of course, a huge literature on judicial restraint, its whys and wherefores. See, for example, Alexander Bickel, *The Supreme Court and the Idea of Progress* (1970); John H. Ely, *Democracy and Distrust* (1980).

[197] For instance, see "The Next Steps in Combating Age Discrimination in Employment: With Special Reference to Mandatory Retirement Policy," working paper prepared for use by the Special Committee on Aging, U.S. Senate, August 1977. The paper stated: "Probably no form of age discrimination in employment is as pernicious or far-reaching in its impact as mandatory retirement" (p. 25). It recommended that Congress take the age cap off ADEA and prohibit "involuntary retirement because of age." See also "Mandatory Retirement: The Social and Human Cost of Enforced Idleness," Report by the Select Committee on Aging, 95th Cong., 1st sess., August 1977.

[198] Public Law 95-256, April 6, 1978 (92 Stat. 189); 5 U.S.C.A. sec. 8335.

[199] *New York Times*, August 19, 1982, p. 13, col. 5: Malcolm Lovell, Jr., Undersecretary of Labor, "urged Congress . . . to approve legislation that would end the forced retirement of elderly workers." The President (Reagan) supported this change in the law, according to Lovell. Indeed, the President had said so in April. But then second thoughts developed, after a certain amount of business pressure. Stephen R. McConnell, "Age Discrimination in Employment," in Herbert S. Parnes, ed., *Policy Issues in Work and Retirement* (1983), p. 185.

[200] Ill. Rev. Stat. 1975, ch. 48, pars. 881–87.

[201] Teale v. Sears, Roebuck and Co., 66 Ill.2d 1, 359 N.E.2d 473 (1976). The court's reasoning was a bit forced. It ignored the word "right" in the statute and stressed the fact that the statute spoke of protecting the right "as provided herein." (They might just as easily have quoted language about construing the act "to effectuate" its "policy.") The court also pointed out that in other states antidiscrimination statutes specifically provided for certain remedies. It would be "incongruous" to derive "by implication" a right to recover "unlimited damages."

In Johnson v. United States Steel Corporation, 348 Mass. 168, 202 N.E.2d 816 (1964), the Massachusetts statute declared a "public policy" against discrimination in hiring or firing. The protected age group was 45 to 65; but the only sanction mentioned was publicity; the commissioner of labor was to publish the name of the offending employer in the newspaper. The court refused to imply further sanctions. This statute, of course, predated ADEA.

[202] Ill. Rev. Stats. ch. 68, pars. 1–101ff. Age discrimination is "unlawful" as to those between the ages of 40 and 70. In fiscal 1982, the Department of Human Rights reported that 176 complaints of age discrimination in employment were received—7 percent of the total. State of Illinois, *Second Annual Report*, Department of Human Rights and Human Rights Commission (1982), p. 20.

[203] Laws Cal. 1977, ch. 851; Cal. Labor Code sec. 1420.15. The private

universities of the state lobbied, successfully, alas, to get tenured faculty members exempted. Laws Cal. 1978, ch. 1190; Laws Cal. 1979, ch. 734. The exception was upheld against constitutional challenge in Lamb v. Scripps College, 627 F.2d 1015 (9th Cir. 1980). Efforts to undo this amendment have not been successful so far.

On the retirement of civil servants, see Cal. Gov't. Code sec. 20983.5, which, except for highway patrolmen and "safety" employees, grants "the right to delay retirement past 70" on "certification of . . . eligibility" by supervisors or department heads.

Since this manuscript was written, the pace of legislation has quickened. According to an article in the *New York Times*, that state was on the brink of abolishing mandatory retirement in May 1984 ("Mandatory Retirements Facing Curbs in Albany," *New York Times*, May 2, 1984, p. B3); both houses had agreed to the bill, and it was waiting for the governor's signature. The Republicans, according to the article, had "blocked measures to outlaw mandatory retirement" until 1984; but they "dropped their objections" after they became satisfied that the business community would not be "burdened with extra costs." The law was to take effect in January 1985, for public employees, and in January 1986, for private workers. The article also claimed that nineteen states had already adopted measures similar to the New York law. California and Connecticut were specifically mentioned.

[204] Under the 1977 law, the starting date for most workers covered by collective bargains or pension plans which had specified a retirement age was extended to two years "after the effective date" of the act, which meant the beginning of 1980. Laws Cal. 1977, ch. 851, Cal. Labor Code 1420.1(a), 1420.15.

[205] Alas. Stats. sec. 18.80.220; enforcement is covered in 18.80.100–30.

[206] 18.80.300(2),(3). The Alaska statute was at issue in Simpson v. Providence Washington Insurance Group, 423 F.Supp. 552 (1976). (This was a federal case because of diversity of citizenship.) Defendant argued that federal law preempted the field; the court disagreed. The employer also argued, rather weakly, that the law "implied" an age limit of 65. The court brushed this aside. The legislature must have known that the word "age" in the law was "open ended," that there were no "restraints on the upper end of the spectrum."

Kennedy v. Community Unit School District No. 7, 23 Ill. App.3d 382, 319 N.E.2d 243 (1974) hinted at a willingnesss to read such a limitation into the Illinois statute. The issue was teacher retirement (at 65). The court relied mainly on the statutory clause excepting "retirement systems" that were not "subterfuges."

[207] 161 N.J. Super. 218, 391 A.2d 558 (1978).

[208] On the Maine law, see Susan D. Kertzer, "Perspectives on Older Workers: Maine's Prohibition of Mandatory Retirement," *Maine Law Review* 33 (1981): 157. The law was pushed by what Kertzer calls a "strong lobby of elderly citizens." Organized labor was neutral and played no part in the battle over the bill. The governor vetoed the act, but the legislature had no trouble overriding his veto.

[209] Public Act No. 78-350-078. The act also prohibited discrimination by employment agencies and labor organizations, and banned discriminatory advertisements.

[210] Talcott Parsons, "The Aging in American Society," *Law and Contemporary Problems* 27 (1962): 22, 30–31.

[211] Ibid., p. 24. The point made in the text holds true *generally*; though

individual bosses might, at times, keep some older workers on at easier jobs. For the great mass of industrial workers, however, retirement was as forever as death, at least as far as their primary job was concerned.

[212] Even among coal miners, there are apparently many people who want to keep working (whether or not they "like" their job). One survey of 166 coal miners in southern Illinois, published in 1954, found that 43 percent valued their jobs for reasons that went beyond money. One miner said: "I would go crazy if I quit. I have to have something to do." Another said: "I don't want to stop working. I'm afraid I'd rot"; still another: "I'd rather wear out than rust out." Eugene A. Friedmann and Robert J. Havighurst, *The Meaning of Work and Retirement* (1954; reprinted, 1977), pp. 88–89.

[213] Disengagement theory was developed in *Growing Old* (1961), by Elaine Cumming and William Henry. The quotation in the text is from Arlie R. Hochschild, "Disengagement Theory: A Critique and Proposal," *American Sociological Review* 40 (1975): 553. See also Robert J. Havighurst, Bernice L. Neugarten, and Sheldon S. Tobin, "Disengagement and Patterns of Aging," in Bernice L. Neugarten, ed., *Middle Age and Aging: A Reader in Social Psychology* (1968), p. 161; Arlie R. Hochschild, "Disengagement Theory: A Logical, Empirical and Phenomenological Critique," in Jaber F. Gubrium, ed., *Time, Roles and Self in Old Age* (1976), p. 53; Richard B. Calhoun, *In Search of the New Old* (1978), pp. 117–25.

[214] Stanley Parker, *Work and Retirement* (1982), p. 58.

[215] See Joel Cooper and George R. Goethals, "The Self-Concept and Old Age," in Sara B. Kiesler et al., *Aging: Social Change* (1981), p. 431.

[216] See Vance v. Bradley, 440 U.S. 93 (1979), which upheld mandatory retirement—at 60—for Foreign Service officers; and compare Schlesinger v. Ballard, 419 U.S. 498 (1975). In that case, a naval lieutenant had twice failed to win promotion to lieutenant commander. He was accordingly dismissed. He complained that a different rule applied to women officers (which was true); the Supreme Court, by a narrow margin (5 to 4), turned down his complaint. The majority found no violation of the due process clause and talked about the navy's need for a "flow of promotions" which would serve to "motivate qualified commissioned officers to so conduct themselves that they may realistically look forward to higher levels of command" (p. 510).

On the constitutionality of the "up-or-out" system in the Foreign Service generally, see Colm v. Kissinger, 406 F.Supp. 1250 (D.C.D.C., 1975). Attacks on its *procedures*, however, have sometimes been successful; see Lindsay v. Kissinger, 367 F.Supp. 949 (S.D.N.Y., 1973).

[217] ADEA, sec. 4(f)(1). Also, under sec. 4(f)(3), the employer can "discharge . . . an individual for good cause."

[218] Marshall v. Arlene Knitwear, Inc., 454 F.Supp. 715 (E.D.N.Y., 1978); see also Geller v. Markham, 635 F.2d 1027 (2d Cir. 1980); cert. den., 101 S.Ct. 2028 (1981).

[219] Mastie v. Great Lakes Steel Corp., 424 F.Supp. 1299, 1319 (E.D. Mich., 1976).

[220] See, for example, Geller v. Markham, 635 F.2d 1027 (1980), discussed on p. 39. In Gill v. Union Carbide Corporation, 368 F.Supp. 364 (E.D. Tenn., 1973), plaintiff lost—there was evidence that the company, which was forced to cut back, because of poor business, actually gave *preference* to workers who had "long company service" and were over 40. See also Williams v. General Motors Corp.,

656 F.2d 120 (5th Cir. 1981), another case of "reduction in force," which the company won.

[221] "The Cost of Growing Old: Business Necessity and the Discrimination in Employment Act," *Yale Law Journal* 88 (1979): 565, 590–93.

[222] Edward P. Lazear, "Why Is There Mandatory Retirement?" *Journal of Political Economy* 87 (1979): 1261. Lazear argues that "workers and firms all benefit from the existence of mandatory retirement." It is the best way to organize the contract between a worker and his firm, assuming that the worker intends to stay with the firm for the long haul. Of course, some soreheads may be "unhappy" when the actual day of retirement draws nigh, but "their lifetime wealth levels" had been increased by being able to "enter into these kinds of contracts." And if society gets rid of mandatory retirement, "there will be an efficiency loss" that will affect "all workers and firms adversely." But see James H. Schulz, "The Economics of Mandatory Retirement," *Industrial Gerontology* 1 (Winter 1974): 1, which argues that there is no clear evidence of economic gain to employers from rules of mandatory retirement.

[223] Robert M. MacDonald, *Mandatory Retirement and the Law* (1978), pp. 18–19.

[224] O'Neil v. Baine, 568 S.W.2d 761 (Mo., 1978). This case also used the "fresh blood" argument: "mandatory retirement increases the opportunity for qualified persons—men and women alike—to share in the judiciary and permits an orderly attrition through retirement." The case is discussed in *"O'Neil v. Baine*: Application of Middle-Level Scrutiny to Old-Age Classifications," *University of Pennsylvania Law Review* 127 (1979): 798.

Historical footnote: the "fresh blood" idea was used by Franklin D. Roosevelt as one justification for his "court-packing plan." In his 1937 message to Congress, Roosevelt wrote that "the modern tasks of judges call . . . for a constant infusion of new blood in the courts." He referred to the "lowered mental and physical vigor" of old judges; "new facts become blurred through old glasses fitted, as it were, for the needs of another generation; older men . . . cease to explore or inquire into the present or the future." Quoted in Peter H. Irons, *The New Deal Lawyers* (1982), p. 276.

The "fresh blood" argument is perhaps the most common argument for retirement. For example, Edward Reinfurt, of Associated Industries of New York, praised compulsory retirement in 1977: it allows both the worker and the employer to plan ahead and brings in "new blood," with "new values, new skills and aggressive personnel" (*New York Times*, January 22, 1977).

[225] William Braithwaite, "Removal and Retirement of Judges in Missouri: A Field Study," *Washington University Law Review* (1968): 378.

[226] Ibid., p. 397.

[227] Stephen Field was appointed in 1863; he was 46 at the time, and he served on the court for more than thirty-four years. In his last year, his health failed markedly, and he was persuaded to resign. Justice Harlan, who had been sent to talk to him, reminded Field that Field had once, as a young justice, performed the same function. Justice Robert C. Grier had suffered a stroke in the late 1860s, and Field persuaded him to step down. Field exclaimed: "A dirtier day's work I never did in my life." Carl B. Swisher, *Stephen J. Field, Craftsman of the Law* (1930), p. 113.

[228] Universities need mandatory retirement to "prevent intellectual stagnation," according to J. Ferguson in Lamb v. Scripps College, 627 F.2d 1015, 1022 (9th

Cir. 1980). A mandatory retirement policy allows a company or municipal agency to "open up more places for new people with fresh ideas." Martin v. Tamaki, 607 F.2d 307, 310 (9th Cir. 1979). Martin, kicked out at 65—alas, before the new California law went into effect—had been a public relations man for the Los Angeles Department of Water and Power, where "fresh ideas" were probably badly needed.

The President of Stanford University, Donald Kennedy, wrote to Senator Donald Nickles of Oklahoma in September 1982, urging that tenured professors be left out of any federal law to get rid of mandatory retirement. He spoke about the need for a "balance" between senior and junior faculty and warned that getting rid of mandatory retirement would hinder the university in its program to add more blacks and women. (A similar warning was sounded by Edward Reinfurt, representing industry in New York, whom we quoted above, *New York Times*, January 22, 1977.) William Bowen, president of Princeton, chimed in with an argument about the need for a "constant influx . . . of fresh ideas and the most recently developed skills, especially in new and developing disciplines" (*Stanford Daily*, October 1, 1982, p. 1).

[229] Pell, J., dissenting in Gault v. Garrison, 569 F.2d 993, 1000 (7th Cir. 1977). This is also a theme of the university moguls cited in the note just above. Often all the arguments are combined; see Mittelstaedt v. Board of Trustees of the University of Arkansas, 487 F.Supp. 960 (E.D. Ark., 1980).

[230] One of these is Bankers Life and Casualty Company, which has always rejected compulsory retirement; its experience goes back over thirty years. In 1977, 4 percent of the workers were over 65, which shows that the policy did not mean that Bankers would become "top-heavy with older workers." It is "very rare" for a problem to arise where a worker "can no longer do the job" and must be retired. (The source of this is a statement presented by Gerald Maguire, vice president of corporate services, House Select Subcommittee on Aging, March 16, 1977.) See also James W. Walker and Harriet L. Lazer, *The End of Mandatory Retirement* (1978), pp. 58–60.

[231] William M. Read, senior vice president, Atlantic Richfield Company, "Reactions to the Elimination of Mandatory Retirement: The Corporate Sector," in *Work, Aging and Retirement*, a report of a convocation sponsored by the Ethel Percy Andrus Gerontology Center, University of Southern California, January 28–30, 1980, p. 26. Read felt that it was "too early to determine the full impact" of getting rid of mandatory retirement. This was because the population was "conditioned" to the idea of retirement at 65, because of strong early retirement benefits, and because high inflation was "only beginning to be felt."

[232] Lawrence M. Friedman, *A History of American Law* (1973), pp. 484–94.

[233] On the labor injunction, see Felix Frankfurter and Nathan Greene, *The Labor Injunction* (1930); Lawrence M. Friedman, *A History of American Law*, pp. 487–88.

[234] Under Flemming v. Nestor, 363 U.S. 603 (1960), the "right" to payments at 65 was held *not* to be truly vested; but even assuming this cold war relic is still living law, the public has tended to assume the pensions were vested in fact.

[235] On the social meaning of "rights," in both an objective and subjective sense, see Lawrence M. Friedman, "The Idea of Right as a Social and Legal Concept," *Journal of Social Issues* 27 (1971): 189.

[236] See H. Laurence Ross and Neil O. Littlefield, "Complaint as a Problem-Solving Mechanism," *Law and Society Review* 12 (1978): 199; Douglas Rosenthal, *Lawyer and Client: Who's in Charge?* (1974).

[237] See, in general, Lawrence M. Friedman, *The Legal System: A Social Science Perspective* (1975).

[238] See Gunther Teubner, "Substantive and Reflexive Elements in Modern Law," *Law and Society Review* 17 (1983): 239.

[239] 21 C.F.R. sec. 152.126.

[240] On the history of workmen's compensation, see Lawrence M. Friedman and Jack Ladinsky, "Social Change and the Law of Industrial Accidents," *Columbia Law Review* 67 (1967): 50.

[241] The Idaho case is Louie v. Bamboo Gardens, 67 Ida. 469, 185 Pac.2d 712 (1947); the Wisconsin case is Karlslyst v. Industrial Commission, 243 Wis. 612, 11 N.W.2d 179 (1943).

[242] Samuel D. Warren and Louis Brandeis, "The Right to Privacy," *Harvard Law Review* 4 (1890): 193.

[243] G. Boglietti, "Discrimination against Older Workers and the Promotion of Equality of Opportunity," *International Labour Review* 110 (1974): 351. According to one source, Private Member bills have been introduced at least four times in the British Parliament; but no age discrimination law has yet passed. Robert Elmore, "The Older Worker and Age Discrimination," *Journal of Business Law* 406 (November 1980).

[244] This is sec. 17, par. 3, of Arbetsraett: L. om Arbetsforhallande (Finnish Code, cited in the Swedish language version).

[245] BetrVerfG, Part IV, sec. 75(1). "Arbeitgeber und Betriebsrat . . . haben darauf zu achten, dass Arbeitnehmer nicht wegen Ueberschreitung bestimmter Altersstufen benachteiligt werden."

[246] For a popular account, see *Maclean's*, March 1, 1982, p. 50; see also Margaret A. Somerville, "Law, Aging and the Elderly," *Legal Medical Quarterly* 241 4 (1980): 242–44.

[247] Ontario Human Rights Code, Stats. of Ont., ch. 318 (1970).

[248] Manitoba Human Rights Commission, 1981 Annual Report, p. 20.

[249] Neb. Rev. Stats. sec. 48-2002. Age discrimination was declared to be "contrary to American principles of liberty and equality of opportunity" and also "incompatible with the Constitution." It also "deprives the State of the fullest utilization of its capacities for production, and endangers the general welfare." Moreover, "bias against workers over forty" wastes an "important resource" and robs older people of "the dignity and status of self-support."

[250] *13th Annual Report, 1979/80, State of Nebraska, Equal Opportunity Commission*, p. 8.

[251] Laws Cal. 1961, ch. 1623, Unemp. Comp. Code, sec. 2070: "It is the public policy of . . . California that manpower should be used to its fullest extent . . . that human beings . . . should be judged fairly and without regard to rigid and unsound rules. . . . Accordingly, use by employers, employment agencies, and labor organizations of arbitrary and unreasonable rules which bar or terminate employment on the ground of age offend the public policy of this State." Sec. 2072 made it "unlawful . . . to refuse to hire . . . or to discharge, dismiss, reduce, suspend or demote any individual between the ages of 40 and 64 solely on the ground of age, except in cases where the law compels or provides for such action."

[252] 1976–78 Annual Report, California FEPC, Tables 1 and 2.

[253] *23rd Annual Report., Ohio Civil Rights Commission, 1982*, p. 5.

[254] Report, 1981–82 [Conn.], *Commission on Human Rights and Opportunities*, p. 28; *Minnesota Department of Human Rights Biennial Report 1981–1982*, p. 6.

[255] *Minnesota Department of Human Rights Biennial Report 1981–1982*, p. 20; *Biennial Report 1979–1980*, p. 15. Virtually all of the complaints were about employment discrimination.

[256] Information supplied by Division of Human Rights, Executive Department, State of New York, June 30, 1980.

[257] Letter from Jimmy Coleman, Field Operations Chief, North Carolina Human Relations Council, July 19, 1983. In 10 of the 22, there was a finding of "no cause." One withdrew, 6 were referred to EEOC, one to "Legal Aid"; there were 3 instances of "administrative closure" and one of "investigative failure." North Carolina, it seems, is no hotbed of claims-conscious workers.

[258] Idaho received 40 complaints in fiscal 1983, July 1982–June 1983; letter from Angela G. Thibodeau, Idaho Human Rights Commission, July 12, 1983. In a two-year period, ending June 30, 1983, the Nevada Equal Rights Commission received 94 complaints; letter from Dorothy Lum, Nevada Equal Rights Commission, August 10, 1983.